	1920	1930	1940	1950	1960	1970	1980	1990	2000	2010
	Greatest		Silent		Boomers		GenX		Gen@	

Generations

THE **CHALLENGE**
OF A **LIFETIME**
FOR **YOUR NONPROFIT**

Peter C. Brinckerhoff

FIELDSTONE
ALLIANCE

SAINT PAUL
MINNESOTA

Fieldstone Alliance is committed to strengthening the performance of the nonprofit sector. Through the synergy of its consulting, training, publishing, and research and demonstration projects, Fieldstone Alliance provides solutions to issues facing nonprofits, funders, and the communities they serve. Fieldstone Alliance was formerly Wilder Publishing and Wilder Consulting departments of the Amherst H. Wilder Foundation. If you would like more information about Fieldstone Alliance and our services, please contact

Fieldstone Alliance
60 Plato Boulevard East, Suite 150
Saint Paul, MN 55107

800-274-6024
www.FieldstoneAlliance.org

Manufactured in the United States of America
First printing, March 2007

Edited by Vincent Hyman
Text and cover designed by Kirsten Nielsen

Library of Congress Cataloging-in-Publication Data

Brinckerhoff, Peter C., 1952-
   Generations : the challenge of a lifetime for your nonprofit / by Peter C. Brinckerhoff. -- 1st ed.
      p. cm.
   "Edited by Vincent Hyman"--T.p. verso.
   Includes index.
   ISBN-13: 978-0-940069-55-8
   ISBN-10: 0-940069-55-5
   1. Nonprofit organizations--Management. 2. Associations, institutions, etc.--Management. 3. Intergenerational relations--Economic aspects. 4. Work ethic. 5. Organizational effectiveness. I. Hyman, Vincent L. II. Title.
   HD62.6.B738 2007
   658'.048--dc22
                                        2006102545

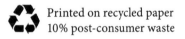
Printed on recycled paper
10% post-consumer waste

Dedication

For my grandchildren, none of whom are born, or even conceived, as I write this. May they inherit a charitable sector as vibrant, as diverse, as energetic, and as committed as the one I have worked with all my life.

Acknowledgements

In the development and writing of this book I talked to dozens of people, and e-mailed and chatted online with dozens more. Many people whose perspective and wisdom I value highly were kind enough to look at early drafts of some or all of the manuscript.

I appreciate all of your input, suggestions, and ideas. You enlightened me about the issues we're facing as a sector, confirmed the magnitude of the challenge, and vastly improved this book.

My thanks go out to each of you.

My thanks also goes to my editor, Vince Hyman. This is our second collaboration, and I marvel at his ability to see through my sloppy thinking and find the real messages I am trying to convey. If you like the book, and find it readable, thank Vince.

About the Author

PETER BRINCKERHOFF is an internationally known expert at helping nonprofits get more mission for their money. Since embarking on his consulting career by forming his firm, Corporate Alternatives, Inc., in 1982, Peter has worked with thousands of nonprofit staff and board members throughout the United States. He is a widely published author with more than fifty articles on nonprofit management in such prominent journals as *Nonprofit World, Advancing Philanthropy, Contributions, Strategic Governance*, and the *Journal of Nonprofit and Voluntary Sector Marketing*. Peter is also the author of the Mission-Based Management series—which includes the books *Mission-Based Management, Financial Empowerment, Social Entrepreneurship, Faith-Based Management*, and the *Mission-Based Management* and *Mission-Based Marketing Workbooks*—and *Nonprofit Stewardship: A Better Way to Lead Your Mission-Based Organization*. Peter's texts are used in graduate and undergraduate nonprofit programs at more than one hundred colleges and universities worldwide.

Peter brings a wide range of practical, hands-on experience to his writing, consulting, and training. He has served as a board member, staff member, and executive director of a number of local, state, and national nonprofits, and understands all three of these perspectives and their importance in the nonprofit mix.

In 2003, Peter was appointed adjunct professor of social enterprise at the Kellogg School of Management at Northwestern University in Evanston, IL. Peter teaches the core course in nonprofit management to MBA students at Kellogg.

Peter received his bachelor's degree from the University of Pennsylvania and his master's in Public Health from the Tulane University School of Public Health.

Peter can be reached online through his web site: www.missionbased.com.

Contents

1

Introduction

WELCOME. I'm glad you've joined me for this exploration of a seismic change in our nonprofit organizations and in our communities—the world that all of us will experience, and that none of us can avoid or escape. As the old Bob Dylan lyric goes, "The times they are a-changin'," and never more rapidly or profoundly than the times we are about to go through.

The most populous generation in history, my generation, the Boomers, are getting ready to . . . to what? To retire from their for-profit jobs? Yes. To start a second career in a nonprofit? Yes. To volunteer more than they've had time to during their work years? Yes. To retire from their nonprofit jobs? Yes. To retire later than our parents did? Probably. To hand off the leadership of our nonprofits to two generations of people that they really don't understand? Yes. To spend a major portion of their lifetime health care costs in the final years of their lives? Yes. To stress out the social fabric of society to the maximum extent possible? Yes. To vote more as they age? Yes.

Read that paragraph again. This time, think about the implications for your nonprofit. Will you have more people to serve in ten years, or fewer? If you don't provide services to the aging part of our population, do you think your funding levels from governmental and foundation sources will drop, stay the same, or increase? How are you going to replace retiring staff and board members, particularly at senior management levels, even as you attempt to get by with fewer administrators and less administrative cost? If you are a Boomer, how will you recruit, retain, and relate to the twenty-somethings (who I call Gen@) and thirty-somethings (GenX) who are quickly becoming your staff and board members? Will the same twenty- and thirty-year-olds be willing to donate as much time, talent, and treasure as the Boomers?

On and on go the questions. When you begin to think about this issue, it gets big and complex in a hurry. I've been pondering it for a number of years, mostly as a result of my own aging (I'm a relatively old Boomer, born in 1952) and from disparate but related questions from nonprofit staff and board members. Here are a few queries that I've fielded many times:

> *"Our board is getting old. We have board terms of office, and we have new board members, but the average age is rising steadily. Seems like ten years ago the average age was about forty-five. Now, it's fifty-five. How can we turn this around?"*

> *"I'm a Boomer, and I made a career change two years ago, coming to this organization as IT manager after twenty-five years at GE. I love what the organization does; it makes me feel like I'm contributing something important to the community. But these people, I can hardly talk to them. They are SO lackadaisical about running this place. It's driving me nuts. What can I do?"*

> *"I'm fifty-five and a twenty-year exec. I have NEVER had more than the normal share of problems with employees, but these twenty-somethings are sending me over the edge. Is it them, or is it me?"*

> *"I came here straight out of graduate school with a master's in nonprofit management. This place was, and still is, in disarray, but I can't get anyone to focus on what's important. It's obvious that they think I'm too young to know anything. Help me!"*

> *"I'm sixty and would like to retire in a couple of years, but there is no one here who I'm comfortable passing the job to, and we've never had (or been allowed to have) enough administrative depth to accommodate a succession plan. I don't want to leave the organization high and dry. What are my options?"*

> *"What is it with the work ethic of the (Boomers, GenXers, twenty-somethings)? I don't get it, or they don't. Whoever is responsible, it's not working!"*

Perhaps you've heard questions like this in your own organization, or coming out of your own mouth. They are not uncommon, and they are only going to be more ubiquitous in the next few years. I researched and wrote this book to answer these questions and dozens of others like them.

What You'll Learn from This Book

This book is written for the *leadership* (volunteer and paid) of nonprofits and nongovernmental organizations (NGOs) worldwide, as well as those people who study and care about the nonprofit sector. The issues we will cover in these pages are universal and not limited to the United States by any means. If you are from Canada, the United Kingdom, continental Europe, or much of East Asia, you have your own baby boom to contend with, your own Gen@ to assimilate, your own financial impacts to respond to. Just because the focus of this book is on the United States does not mean that the phenomenon stops at its shores. It is, for a large part of the developed world, the same large issue with local variations.

If you are a board member, trustee, midmanager, senior manager, executive director, funder, capacity builder, or policy maker, there is important and relevant material in this book for you.

As readers of my other books well know, I feel that you are investing time with me, and I want to be sure you get the most return on that investment possible. So, here's what you'll get for your investment in this book, whether you are just browsing at this point or are ready to get into the issues in depth.

By the time you have finished this book, you will

- Understand why planning for and managing generation change is crucial to your nonprofit and its continued ability to provide high-quality mission in your community.

- Know the steps to deal with generation change in a variety of areas from human resources to marketing to technology to management.

- Have a start on your generation benchmarks, and be ready to incorporate generational issues into your strategic, financial, and marketing plans.
- Be aware of generational differences and similarities in managing across generation lines.
- Be better prepared to make the best of the opportunities generational change affords your organization.

A User's Guide

Here's a quick tour of the book and how to get the most out of it.

Most chapters are set up in the same format. The introductory paragraphs lay out the issues to be covered in the chapter, followed by a number of sections dealing with the chapter's topic. You will regularly find text labeled **FOR EXAMPLE**. These provide relevant examples to explain and amplify a point. You'll also find text labeled **HANDS ON,** with ideas that you can use immediately.

Most chapters end with a summary that reviews the key points and a set of discussion questions that will help you and your team review and follow up on ideas.

The goal of this book is change, and you can't make changes alone. Consider using this book with an interested group of staff and board members—in this case, trying your best to be sure that group has a mix of generations represented. Or you might create a learning circle around the book, discussing the chapter questions with your peers in other organizations.

Now, let's look at the chapters themselves.

Chapter 1. Introduction

This is the chapter you are now reading. It includes some introductory material, a definition of who the book is designed for, a user's guide to the book, and some closing suggestions. The rest of this book is split into two parts, Part One: Where We Are and Part Two: Where We're Going.

PART ONE: Where We Are

Part One consists of two chapters that prepare you for changes you'll need to make. These two chapters lay out the key facts about generational change, including the scope and size of the issue and its relevance to your nonprofit.

Chapter 2. Change Is Upon Us

Jim Collins, in *Good to Great,* notes that great organizations share a characteristic of "facing the brutal facts." This chapter gives you those facts—at least as they relate to demographics. While the facts and trends in this chapter may not be brutal, they are daunting and a wake-up call for all of us. After reading this chapter, you won't need any caffeine for the rest of the day.

Chapter 3. Generations and Your Organization

This chapter connects the data about generational change with day-to-day management, organizational planning, and strategy. It poses challenges: Do you understand what generational change is doing to your organization now? Do you understand what it will be doing in the next ten years? Are you ready? And, just to be sure that you don't try to avoid those questions, there's a generational organizational self-assessment tool at the end of the chapter.

PART TWO: Where We're Going

With facts and their impact in hand, it's time for you to figure out how to respond. Part Two offers hands-on ideas on how to deal with generation issues as they affect each domain of your organization—staff, board, volunteers, clients, and so forth.

Chapter 4. Generations on Staff

Generational differences on staff have always been a challenge, and never more so than today. In this chapter, we'll look at recruitment, retention, supervision, incentives, and team issues for Boomers, GenXers, Gen@s, and recently retired for-profit or public sector workers who are seeking a second, more meaningful, career. We'll also examine whether you need to rethink fringe benefits plans, work hours, dress codes, and access to technology. Here's a question to vex you: What's your iPod policy?

Chapter 5. Board and Volunteers

Old board, young board—what's the balance? Different skills and "offers" are required to recruit and retain younger and older board members. Managing the expectations of these different groups, as well as benefiting from the skills of retired Boomers, will be covered in detail in this chapter.

Chapter 6. The People You Serve

Since mission—the people you serve—is the *reason* you are in business, generational impact is key. This chapter helps you accommodate your services to older and younger populations *simultaneously*. With people at both ends of the age spectrum (and in the middle) changing in different ways, it becomes even more important to remain alert and flexible. This chapter will show how to look for ways to do that.

Chapter 7. Marketing to Generations

How do you keep in touch with the young, the middle-aged, and the "less young"? How do you determine what they want? How will the next ten years affect the way you discover wants and let people know about your mission, services, and organization? How do you deal with "MeBranding"? This chapter will help you accommodate your marketing approaches to both generational and technological change.

Chapter 8. Generations and Technology

Technology is crucial to managing generational change. But key questions need to be answered in a rational order, not just pell-mell: How can we use technology to bridge the generation gap? What are the uses of technology to improve our appeal to both the young and the older worker or volunteer? How can we avoid having technology divide us from each other and the people we serve? Like it or not, technology is here to stay, so we'll answer these questions and more in this chapter.

Chapter 9. Financial Implications

Change carries costs and benefits. What does generational change mean for your organization's finances? This chapter examines issues such as the inevitable burden on benefits and retirement funds, and the need to carefully consider the future of pension plans if you have them. Other financial effects that accompany generational changes include recruitment and retention funds, accommodations to older workers, and technology overhauls. Does "aging down" the average age of workers mean lower salary costs over time? Or is the expectation of new, highly trained nonprofit managers that they will earn a better living than their predecessors?

Resources

This section includes a wide array of follow-up resources, including books, workbooks, online articles, organizations, and web sites. You will also find a special web site just for readers of the book.

Summary

A friend of mine once told me what his grandfather used to say about getting in the way of big changes: "The train is leaving the station. You can be on it, or under it."

While a bit harsh, there is a lot of truth in his admonition. Demographics are a huge predictor of and influence on social change, work habits, and community needs. As such, they will affect your organization and all of its good works. The fact that you've picked up this book is a good sign that you have recognized this issue as one that is central to the future of your organization's mission.

But, in many ways, that future is already here, and we don't have time to waste. So, in Collins's words, let's turn to "the brutal facts." That's the subject of our next chapter.

PART ONE

Where We Are

What is it with the work ethic of the (Boomers, GenXers, twenty-somethings)? I don't get it, or they don't. Whoever is responsible, it's not working!

I'm a Boomer, and I made a career change two years ago, coming to this organization as IT manager after twenty-five years at GE. I love what the organization does; it makes me feel like I'm contributing something important to the community. But these people, I can hardly talk to them. They are SO lackadaisical about running this place. It's driving me nuts. What can I do?

Things are changing so fast in our community; it's becoming a blur. I thought I had a handle on growth, on need, on our position in relation to our peer organizations. No more.

2

Change Is Upon Us

IN THIS CHAPTER, we'll examine some definitions used throughout the book, starting by defining each generation and its unique characteristics.

Next, we'll explore what the change in generations means in terms of overall trends, translating hard numbers into understandable and meaningful movements at the national level, and how that looks through the lens of your mission.

Finally, we'll take a quick look at the impact of these trends on the United States in terms of economy, infrastructure, and other measures of change. These impacts, while not all specific to nonprofits (we'll look at those in detail in Chapter 3), do have effects on the communities we serve, work, and live in.

Who Are We Really Talking About?

As I researched this book, I was intrigued with the range of descriptions regarding different generations. For example, some authors have the Baby Boom starting in 1942 and going to 1965. Others start in 1946, 1947, or 1948. These starting and ending dates change the size of the generation, as well as the scope and timing of its impact. This variance in definitions is present in all the definitions I uncovered.

That said, these differences are just matters of degree. The larger issues related to each generation overwhelm the minutiae, and become the backbone of what we'll look at in relation to your nonprofit organization and its future.

What you will see in the next few pages is really the generational framework as I have decided to use it, and as I have interpreted it. We may disagree about dates and numbers of people in a particular generation, but the larger issues still are valid.

Greatest Generation
(also known as the GI Generation)

Born: 1901–1924.

Size in United States in 2005: Approximately 20 million, but losing thousands of members each month.

Key events: This generation was born in high times, experienced the Great Depression, watched the New Deal take shape, fought and won World War II, and then came home to build the strongest economy in history while also giving birth to the Baby Boomers.

Key values: Financial security, patriotism, belief in the power of institutions, respect for authority, selflessness.

Critical technological change in their lives: Rural electrification, commercial radio.

When working with this generation, focus on: Tradition, helping others, being part of a large-scale, valuable change.

Silent Generation

Born: 1925–1945.

Size in United States in 2005: Approximately 30 million.

Key events: Most of this generation missed serving in World War II, but lived through it as children and adolescents who matured in the 1950s. They grew up with a military draft, came of age during the tension of the Cold War, experienced a long period of social stability and family unity, and then experienced significant disenchantment when the Vietnam War and the Watergate scandal challenged their core beliefs about authority. Over 40 percent of the men in this generation served in the military, and they believe in top-down control and centralized decision making.

Key values: Loyalty, self-sacrifice, stoicism, faith in institutions, intense patriotism.

Critical technological change in their lives: The spread of private automobile ownership, use of early office "machines," massive industrialization.

When working with this generation, focus on: Tradition, loyalty to a key issue in their lives, value of joint work ethic.

Note: While Greatest Generation and Silent Generation members are, thankfully, still with us, still donating time, talent, and treasure, and still enriching our lives and our communities, they are rapidly decreasing in number, and therefore I won't spend a great deal of time on them in the remainder of the book, with the exception of Chapter 6: The People You Serve. That is NOT to suggest I am unaware of the huge debt we in the nonprofit sector owe them—I am.

Baby Boomers (Boomers)

Born: 1946–1962.

Size in United States in 2005: Approximately 80 million.

Key events: This generation, the largest in U.S. history (particularly when you consider the size of the U.S. population in relation to the Boomers while they were being born), grew up in an era of huge social change, but in a wealthy nation, often overindulged by their parents. Because of the Cold War, Boomers, until they were well into their adulthood, lived in a world that might be snuffed out in a day. They were the first generation in nearly 200 years to rebel openly against their government, and nearly every social, scientific, and cultural institution underwent significant change during their adolescence.

Key values: Sense of entitlement, optimism, cynicism about institutions, competition, focused on career, endless youth.

Critical technological change in their lives: Television. In 1952 there were 4 million privately owned televisions. By the turn of the next decade there were over 50 million.

When working with this generation, focus on: Their value to the team, your need for them, their ability to improve your services, that your workplace is young and "cool." Publicly recognize them whenever possible. Tell them that they can help "change the world" by working with you.

Generation X (GenX)

Born: 1963–1980.

Size in United States in 2005: Approximately 45 million (only slightly more than half the number of Boomers).

Key events: This generation has always worked in the shadow of the Boomers, who in many cases held GenXers' careers back because they filled up all the jobs and refused to retire. GenXers are interested in stability, but that does not translate into the idea of staying with one organization. GenXers are confident, but very focused on their career path, even early in employment.

Key values: Independence, self-reliance, desire for stability, informality, fun.

Critical technological change in their lives: Rise of the personal computer, cable TV, and video games.

When working with this generation, focus on: Their value to the work of the organization, the value of independent thinking, your organization's focus on work-life balance.

Gen@

(also known as GenY, Generation Me, or Millennials)

Born: 1981–2002.

Size in United States in 2005: Approximately 75 million (almost the size of the Boomer generation).

Key events: These children of Boomers are the first generation born into a true high-tech society, and they are hardwired to the Internet. They are civic minded, even more than their parents, and have a value structure that includes lifelong learning, and a work-life balance. More than any other generation in American history, they are wired for collaboration and for working in groups.

Another way to define this generation is to look at the people they went to school with and saw on television: *everybody*. More than any generation in American history, Gen@ has had a diverse educational experience. And not just racially, although that is crucial. Gen@ is also the first generation to go to school with people of all disabilities, and to see real ethnic diversity in action in advertising, television, and, most important, in political and business leadership positions. This is not to say that there are no racial divisions and tensions in Gen@. There are. But while Boomers at this age might have said "Some of my best friends are black . . ." and been stretching the facts, for Gen@ multiracial groups, having friends from multiracial homes, and seeing the world as a naturally multiracial environment is so common as to be invisible.

Key values: Work-life balance, confidence, social commitment, *complete* comfort with technology, networking, realism, well-informed, *superb* time managers.

Critical technological change in their lives: The connection between the personal computer and the Internet, with an added dose of the rapid pace of technological advances and innovation. They grew up, and remain, connected.

When working with this generation, focus on: The good that they *and their peers* can do by working with you, the challenge of doing good in the community and doing it well, the need for their new perspective and ideas.

That's a thumbnail sketch of each generation. In later chapters we'll return to, and expand on, how to work with each generation, but first we need to look at the larger trends and what their impact may be on your community, your life, and your organization.

Generational Trends

Let's look at the overarching trends for the next decade that arise from generational change. As noted earlier, we'll look at specific and detailed effects on your nonprofit in the next chapter, but here we need to start by identifying the key generational trends you'll be wrestling with. They include

- Financial stress
- Technological acceleration
- Diversity of population
- Redefining the family
- MeBranding
- Work-life balance

Financial stress

News flash: There's not enough money, and it's primarily a generational thing. Here's why.

The impending retirement of the Boomers will screw everything up. In societies like the United States, Great Britain, Japan, and Europe, the social safety net will be bulging with retirees who need to be supported by GenX and Gen@ workers. Remember the Boomers' sense of entitlement? Well, watch it go to work here. Not only are there 80 million Boomers, but as people age, they tend to vote more, and Boomers *love* a cause . . .

particularly when it revolves around them. Look for government money to continue to move toward issues of importance to Boomers.

More than just government money is moving toward the Boomers. People who watch the demographic trends are telling us that the Boomers will start drawing money out of their retirement funds soon, affecting the stock market, banking, and other financial institutions. Most experts predict that the "tipping point" for this is 2008; some say as late as 2012. That's the time when Boomer contributions to their retirement funds are expected to be smaller than Boomer withdrawals. This means less money in the financial markets, and *nobody* really knows what that will mean. But no one disputes the fact that that day is rapidly approaching.

Federal deficits keep rising as does the incomprehensibly big federal debt. Even if we were to balance the federal budget starting this year, the debt is so big that it limits our options in the near and far term. Why? Well, here's a sobering fact. As I write this in January 2006, the United States is paying just over $48 million *per hour* in *interest* alone. That's right, per hour. And this is just interest: just the cost of the debt, not any contribution to its retirement. Think about that in relation to your organization's annual budget. In how many minutes is it spent? Think of the social, economic, educational, health, and environmental good we could do with that money. With a preponderance of federal (and pass-through state) funding in the nonprofit sector, this is a big issue.

Technological acceleration

You may be sick of reading about the ever-accelerating pace of change, particularly in terms of technology. But the trends here are inescapable: our dependence on, use of, and expectations regarding technology are only going to grow, and grow at an increasing rate. We are going to live in a world where we are "on" all the time, and at a lower and lower cost. You can see this trend most easily in telephony. Anyone over the age of thirty-five can remember worrying about running out of minutes on their cell phones, can recall cell phones being luxuries—families had one for road trips—and can even remember considering something called "long distance" when making a call. Not now. Our family pays less for three phones with no long-distance fees and essentially unlimited minutes—we have not gone over our allotment of 1.3 gazillion minutes in years—than we did for one cell phone eight or nine years ago.

How are we more dependent on technology? It has been said of FedEx that its initial business plan was based on our tendency to procrastinate, while at the same time not wanting to get caught doing so. With the advent of "absolutely, positively guaranteed" overnight delivery, we could accomplish both. Today, in just seconds, we can e-mail someone a document that they need right, *right* now; we can call their cell phone and talk to them nearly anywhere on the planet right, *right* now. Both cases absolve us of planning ahead the way we used to have to.

> **FOR EXAMPLE:** I recently was talking to a friend who had just put his seventeen-year-old daughter on a plane to New York to spend a weekend with her brother at his college. He was shaking his head and told me, "I can't believe their lack of planning. As we pulled up to the airport, I asked my daughter, 'Have you talked to your brother about where you are going to meet him?' She looked at me strangely and said, 'No . . . I'll just call him when the plane lands.'" Thus the brother could be reached in a moving car by his sister sitting on a moving plane to coordinate a meeting location at the last possible minute at LaGuardia.

This kind of last-minute "transaction" is played out hundreds of thousands of times per hour now in homes, in workplaces, before dinners, even at staff and board meetings. And it is wonderful—when it works. Last-possible-minute dependence like this also has a huge downside: when the system goes down, or your individual phone/computer/PDA breaks, you are so, so screwed. Just look at what happened in the aftermath of Hurricane Katrina in the U.S. Gulf states in 2005. A key element of the federal, state, and local response plans was the use of cell phones by rescue and response personnel. When the entire cell system in two states went down, people were completely cut off.

We are dependent in other ways on technology—businesses scale up based on their ability to process huge numbers of transactions or customers automatically. Often this brings about increased economies, and just as often it brings risks if the lights go out or the hard drive fails.

The most important trend that's resulted from technological change is *the expectation that we are available and reachable twenty-four hours a day, seven days a week.* For Boomers, this is a really mixed blessing. We are the workaholic generation, so being able to work everywhere is a benefit. But, as we move past fifty-five and sixty, we are more and more bothered by the cell phone ringing at the next table or airline seat, and by the lack of being able to *take a break.* For GenX this is not anywhere near the big deal it is for Boomers, and Gen@ asks, "What's the problem?" This is the way they are wired and this is their expectation for everyone, including Boomers—to be always online and to respond *immediately.*

> **FOR EXAMPLE:** A recent news story mirrors conversations I've had with Boomer CEOs over the past three years. A Boomer exec in the private sector was telling the reporter what it was like to work with Gen@. "What gets me most is how fast they move and how quickly they want answers. I'll walk into my office at 8:30 and have a voice message from a twenty-five-year-old employee that was recorded at 8:15. At 8:45 I'll get my second e-mail from the employee telling me to listen to the voice message, and if I don't respond, before 9:00 they'll stop by to see what the holdup on my answer is. The idea that I might not listen to my voice mail or check my e-mail every three minutes is *completely foreign* to them."

The technology trend, for better or worse, is one that we have to wrestle with, and the key here is that the generations see tech through very, very different lenses. For the Boomers, we view tech through bifocals—seeing tech as good and bad. For GenX, tech is viewed through tinted lenses: How can I color tech to work for me? For Gen@, tech isn't viewed—it's invisible, like the atmosphere they breathe. They don't even really notice the specific technology, they just consider it a natural part of the landscape, part of their biome. And that is critically important to remember when you consider serving, employing, seeking voluntary help, soliciting donations, or marketing to Gen@.

Diversity of population

Earlier in this chapter I noted that Gen@ is the most diverse generation ever. That is just the generation-specific outcome of a much larger national trend—a much, much more diverse population. In the United States, the Hispanic population, because of both immigration and higher birth rates, is growing at twice the national rate. Sometime in this century (estimates vary on when, but all put it before 2100), Caucasians in the United States will become a minority. Immigration from every corner of the globe continues to swell our population. This is causing some major rethinking for policy makers on national, state, and local levels.

> **FOR EXAMPLE:** Beardstown, Illinois, was a classic small rural farming town. Located on the Illinois River about forty miles northwest of Springfield, it served as a grain shipping center and county seat. In 1978, when I first visited Beardstown, its population was 99.99 percent white. In 1985, nothing had changed. By 2001, the Cass County school system, which serves Beardstown, had started providing English as a second language classes, the local paper was printed in English and Spanish, Spanish-speaking churches were growing, and the local cable operator was considering offering TeleMundo, a Spanish cable channel. In fifteen years, Beardstown went from essentially 100 percent Caucasian to a Hispanic population of nearly 18 percent. And here's the key: *In the age cohort below forty, the Hispanic population was just under 30 percent.*

> What happened? Local crops had changed, and with that change emerged the need for more year-round agricultural workers. First in small groups, then in large families, Hispanic workers from Texas, Mexico, and Central America made their way to Beardstown and the surrounding area. Did this change the shape, the scope, and the culture of this small town? Of course. Did it put new demands on everyone providing services? Absolutely.

Diversity is an issue for all nonprofits, not just those in urban areas, on the coasts, or on the southern U.S. border.

In addition to traditional concepts of racial diversity, other things are going on. More diverse communities lead to more diverse romances. Interracial marriages in the United States are at an all-time high, and the children of these marriages are facing all kinds of questions about cultural identity and where they "belong." While on one level this just gives census takers fits, on another much more important plane self-identity, cultural competence, family traditions, and related cultural identifiers are all in flux, sometimes for the better, sometimes not. We'll examine this more in the next section.

Expect this trend to continue, and to continue to change in its shape, scope, and direction. For example, the influx of highly educated and skilled workers from India to the United States has changed. Once a highly desirable destination for physicians, engineers, and graduate students, the United States is now seen as less desirable. Why? Because India has raced into the twenty-first century, become more politically stable, and developed a booming economy. Jobs abound for the well-trained, educational opportunities are growing, and thus, in 2003 for the first time, the migration flow of Indians between the United States and India *was back to India,* not toward the United States.

Expect changes in diversity. Be flexible.

Redefining the family

I'm not going on a rant—conservative or liberal—about what a family should or should not be. As service providers we have to deal with what families *are,* and here we look at the trends of what families *will become.* One parent or two, two generations or ten, families still are the center of life for most of us, and this will not change. But what *is* changing will affect the way we do our work in the nonprofit sector.

First, families are more mobile, and in new ways. In the last century families moved too—African-American families moved from the South to the North after World War II, Great Plains families moved to California to escape the Dust Bowl, and all kinds of families migrated from cities to suburbs. But when they moved, *they moved together.* The grandparents, children, and grandchildren went as one (or went separately over time as money allowed) in order to keep the proximate family intact.

Today, not so much. Over the past twenty-five years—within the past two generations—we have seen an unprecedented spreading out of families, and here's the key: *the higher the education level, the more likely this is.*

> **FOR EXAMPLE:** Let's use my family as an example. My mother had two siblings and none of the three of them ever lived more than sixty miles from their parents or each other. In fact, when I ran the numbers, the average distance was around thirty-five miles. Then I looked at a map and discovered that the average distance of *my* generation (me, my sister, and six cousins on my mother's side of the family) from our parents is just over 430 miles—and that does not take into account one cousin who recently returned from five years in Africa as a missionary, but now lives 600 miles away from his mother.
>
> What about the next generation? Well, the average for the four kids in my children's generation who have "left home" is over 700 miles from those homes, topped by my son Ben, who lives in Seattle. And looking at the others in Ben's peer group, I see a growing trend. Of Ben's fifteen to twenty closest high-school friends, not one lives within 100 miles of Springfield, and most live more than 500 miles away. My daughter Caitlin's dream job is in Paris, while my son Adam wants to work in Australia for at least a few years. And we're a tight-knit family that gets along and enjoys each other's company!

Becoming and remaining long-distance families has been enabled by technology (fast and cheap air travel, low-cost telephony, and e-mail), and this may be a good thing. But it has changed the long-term, multigenerational commitment to a particular community *and its nonprofits.* It has shortened the time needed to become accepted (at least in many communities). You no longer have to have three generations of ancestors buried in the local cemetery to consider yourself a resident. It has changed the need for day care—if grandma is 400 miles away, you can't drop the kids off with her. It has increased the need for the famous "village" to help raise our children. And as a society, we've not yet figured out the ultimate impact of all of this.

Second, the nature of family itself has changed. With more divorces and remarriages, the number of "steps" in any given house (stepbrother, step-father, and so forth) has exploded. No one knows the implications of this (whether it is bad, good, or neutral is the subject of fierce and very politically charged debate). When you add same-sex marriage, multiple generations, and single parenting into the mix, the definition of family is rapidly changing.

> **FOR EXAMPLE**: In a recent management book discussion group, one participant told me that she was really having to cut slack for most of her midlevel managers, all of whom are in their early to midthirties. "Why?" I asked. "Well, all of them are caring for their grandchildren while their daughters finish high school."

The issue of family change has repercussions on health care benefits, social security, generational legacies, and in a dozen other areas, many of which we're just discovering. But again, we need to expect rapid change. We have to pay attention and keep working on responding to this important trend.

MeBranding

Your spouse gives you a grocery list and you head for the store. On the list are four things: 2 percent milk, tomato soup, yogurt, and mustard. You walk inside, head for the milk. Not a difficult choice. Two percent milk is 2 percent, and soon, the milk is in the cart. Then you head for mustard in the next aisle. Whoa. Who knew there were twenty-three kinds of mustard? So you muse for a bit, make your choice, and move to the yogurt. And stand there staring blankly. To simply read the title of each yogurt choice could take you twenty minutes. Want to find just plain tomato soup? Good luck. You'll have to browse through ten other tomato-plus combinations.

It's not just groceries. How many choices of deodorant, shampoo, coffee, cell phones, even light bulbs assault you when you enter a store? (I'm waiting for a 60-watt toffee-hazelnut bulb to come out.) The proliferation of choice in all aspects of our lives can be beneficial, but it's also often overwhelming. Try walking into a store like Best Buy to choose a flat screen television. Pity the Medicare-eligible seniors who have to choose from forty or fifty different prescription drug plans. Good luck finding plain vanilla ice cream.

If it were just an overload of choices, we could probably cope. The Net allows us to go online to find reviews of products from actual users, to study specs before we buy, even to order something without a pesky salesperson breathing down our neck. Choice is good, but when you add ultracustomization, you begin a social trend with immense impact.

Ultracustomization is the idea that we can segment markets down to the ultimate limit—the individual consumer. I call this "MeBranding." When I can go online and design and order a one-of-a-kind running shoe just for me, that's MeBranding. When I can go to iTunes and download just the music I want, mix it just the way I want, and listen to it to the exclusion of all the other bothersome noise called "the world," that's MeBranding. When I can order a cup of coffee with five adjectives in front of the word "coffee"—*and a company builds its business model around that fact*—that's MeBranding. When I can watch "You're Right!" news, read a "You're Right!" newspaper or magazine, that's MeBranding.

What does this mean, and why should you care? First and foremost, this trend reinforces a level of selfishness and egocentricity that can be very harmful, particularly for young people who know no other world than having it their way all the time. Second, exposure to a *broad and diverse* swath of ideas, music, art, commentary, and information is crucial in a shrinking and more complex world. If I only watch news on FOX and never CNN or BBC or Al-Jazeera, if I only read the *Washington Post* and never the *Washington Times,* if I only go to conservative (liberal, libertarian) web sites and blogs,[1] if I only listen to jazz (or ska, or punk rock, or country) and never to other music, how will I understand the people I live next to, or work with, or serve?

MeBranding can reinforce the sense that "it's all about me all the time." Think of the cell-phone user in a restaurant at the table next to you who yells into his phone for twenty minutes while you are trying to have a quiet dinner. It's all about him. The driver behind you who is honking at you

---

[1] A few readers may be unfamiliar with the term *blog*. It is short for *web log*, an online journal or diary, often inviting response from readers.

for going *only* the speed limit because *she* got up late and is going to be in trouble with her boss? It's all about her.

Now think about MeBranding in relation to nonprofits. What is the core of nonprofit service? Of nonprofit volunteerism? Of nonprofit mission? It's this: It's NOT about us. It's about someone else. How will MeBranding affect our recruitment of staff and volunteers or securing donations?

Most nonprofits offer an array of services, but not ultracustomized ones— we don't have the money or the infrastructure for that. What will MeBranding mean to our ability to provide services that people actually want and are happy with, as opposed to those they just tolerate?

This is mostly (but not completely) a Gen@ issue, with a smattering of GenX included. Boomers are certainly not exempt from being self-centered, but mostly we tend to stand confused and overwhelmed in the face of a shelf full of mega choices, while Gen@ kids just dive in.

Choice is terrific and an anchor of capitalism. But we may have microsegmented our way into a social situation that we will regret.

Work-life balance

This is almost purely a generational issue. As one columnist in *Newsweek* recently put it, Boomers, facing "their final exam," are rethinking their work-life balance as they enter their late fifties and early sixties. Many are coming from the for-profit and government sectors to work and volunteer for nonprofits. Boomers have been the "Thank God It's Monday" generation—working, working, working. They developed the clueless child care rationalization of "quality time," nearly eliminated the idea of a two-week vacation, and started their work life with the belief that every woman could have both a high-end business career *and* be a perfect mother and wife.

Our kids, the Gen@ generation, watched us, as did our younger brothers and sisters, the GenXers, and said, "No way." Don't believe me? Try using this diagram that I first saw in the excellent book *The Leadership Engine* by Noel Tichy.[2] Imagine three circles, one representing work, one representing

---

[2] Noel Tichy and Eli Cohen, *The Leadership Engine: How Winning Companies Build Leaders at Every Level* (New York: HarperBusiness, 1997).

family, and one representing self. The circles should be sized relative to the space you devote to them in your life, and the amount they intersect should reveal the degree to which these elements are integrated. To illustrate, the first diagram below shows a life in which work, self, and family all receive equal attention and also overlap. One could imagine here a person who works in a family business. The second diagram shows a person who does not put a lot of time into family, and who puts work ahead of personal needs.

HANDS ON: Take the three circles "Work," "Family," and "Life," and resize them to fit how you view your life. Have every Boomer in your organization do the same (anonymously). Then have every Gen@ person do it. Compare the results and you will see a BIG difference.

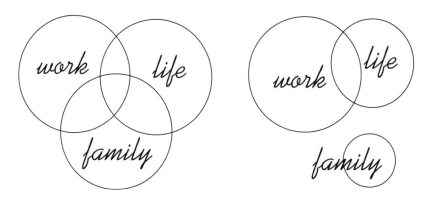

HANDS ON: If you REALLY want to have fun, draw your diagram and then ask your family to draw *your* diagram too. The difference in how you see yourself and how they see you may be a bit sobering. It was for me, and I reevaluated my work versus family time afterwards.

This wonderful trend to rebalance lives and priorities has other ramifications. More highly trained women are dropping out of the career track to stay home and raise children—and more men are making the choice to be stay-at-home dads when their wives have higher earning potential. I read recently that thousands of stay-at-home moms, many armed with MBAs, have started businesses on eBay, with the result that they make more money than at their full-time job, and are much, much happier.

More people want to work from home, or even from remote locations, a trend that is, like the eBay mom, enabled by technology. My son's team at Microsoft's Redmond, Washington, headquarters has one member whose wife took a job near Washington, DC—he now simply works from the East Coast. Two other team members live in, and work from, China. We can expect such arrangements to become increasingly common as employers adapt, commutes lengthen, fuel prices rise, and time becomes more valuable. This is a trend that's not going away.

So, there are the six key trends: financial stress, technological acceleration, diversity of population, redefining the family, MeBranding, and work-life balance. No doubt other important trends affect you and your nonprofit. But these six are critically important to nonprofits and they all have deep generational foundations.

The Impact of Generations

What will be the impact of all these trends? Of course, no one *really* knows. In every area noted above, we have experts making both dire and optimistic predictions. "The end of the world is nigh" and "A new nirvana is dawning": you can sometimes read both headlines in the same week. "We're facing a worldwide depression!" "No, globalization will solve everything." "Technology will lead us to a new level of worldwide community." "Technology will remove our humanity."

So, go figure, right? It would be easy to throw up our hands and say, "Well, we can't change things, so we'll just have to wait and see . . ."

Can't change things? Wait a minute. If you think you can't change things then why do you work for or with a nonprofit? We *exist* to change things, to make things better. So let's leave the disempowerment at the door.

Additionally, as nonprofit board and staff, we are stewards of the resources our community has entrusted to us. Our job is to look out and focus on trends, weigh possible impacts, and then relate them to our resources, our services, our mission. While we can't change these trends, we must be prepared to adapt to them. And while trend experts may disagree about the interpretation of the demographic facts and their impact on us, we must still take our best shot at understanding the data and predicting its impact. We know more about our mission, our community, our organization than anyone else. We're the real experts.

So, let's look at the generational impact of each trend noted above, and consider the difficult questions these impacts raise.

Financial stress

Readers of my other books know that my first rule for nonprofits is *Mission, Mission, Mission!* and the second rule is *No money, no mission*. Whether we like it or not, money is the key to being able to act on our mission. Any trend that affects the flow of money into our organizations is one to attend to. The aging of the Boomers will skew the flow of government, insurance, and private funds toward Boomer issues for the next twenty years (at a minimum). Here are some related finance questions.

- Are we providing any service that relates to Boomer issues? Will the funding for this service increase or will it remain set?

- If the stock market begins a long decline (as Boomers pull money out of their retirement funds), what will the impact be on our endowment, the portfolios and funding ability of foundations, and the giving habits of our wealthier donors?

- With large health care costs coming in the last years of life, what will be the impact of Boomer aging on our health care insurance premiums?

- What kind of retirement options can we provide to younger workers if Social Security benefits are reduced?

- Is ramping up our development effort a viable option to offset reduced or static federal, state, and local funding over the next ten years?

- If GenX and Gen@ workers have a different work-life-balance priority, how will we pay to get the work done? In other words, if they are only willing to work fifty hours a week instead of sixty, how does the work get done, and how do we pay for it?

Technological acceleration

We're in the age where there is no room for Luddites. Technology is with us, and will continue to be more and more important to our marketing, our fundraising, our operations, our transparency, and our ability to provide efficient and effective services. We can and must find tech applications that help Boomers stay engaged as they age, and equally important, we must look at technology not as a luxury, but as a mission-serving tool. The GenX and Gen@ workers and volunteers are getting more and more frustrated with Boomer boards and management resisting using tech to the max. Boomers: Remember when you were frustrated with your parents' not understanding your music? Remember your distrust of authority? Transfer that emotion to your younger workers and *your* attitudes about tech.

Some questions to ponder:

- Technology moves so fast. How can we stay abreast of tech changes, get our work done, and stay within budget?

- Who inside (or outside) of the organization can we find to be an "applied technologist"—someone who looks at our mission, our operations, and our needs, and applies technology to help? Can we get a group of insiders and outsiders to fill this function?

- Technology is an accelerator, not a solution in and of itself (something we'll talk about at length in Chapter 8). So, what functions can we use tech to accelerate? How can we find out and keep abreast of what our peer organizations and our competitors are doing in this area?

- How do we balance the tech needs, wants, and acceptance levels of different generations?

Diversity of population

This book is ultimately about improving your *generational* diversity in addition to ethnic and gender diversity.

As our society continues to become more ethnically complex, nonprofits will face new pressures and challenges at the staff and board level. The generational issues here? Gen@ doesn't see the problem *as* a problem, while Boomers of all backgrounds (who grew up during the era of civil rights, "Black is beautiful," women's rights, and other movements) are hypersensitive to the issue. Additionally, there is a cyclical backlash against immigration (the cycle is usually about twenty years) where some people try to close our borders. That can lead to intolerance, racism, and funding cuts for those who serve immigrant populations. This cycle will persist. It's been going on since the Puritans. No reason to get smart now.

> **FOR EXAMPLE**: While this book was being finished, the U.S. House of Representatives passed an immigration reform bill that would have made it a felony to aid, in any way, an illegal immigrant. Thus, if your nonprofit provided health care, food, housing, counseling, or any other service to any illegal immigrant, you would be guilty of breaking the law. Demonstrations broke out across the United States and fortunately, cooler heads in the Senate prevailed.

Here are some questions to consider related to diversity.

- How is our community becoming more diverse? What dependable data do we have?

- Is anyone at our local colleges and universities or in our local or county government looking out ten years in this area?

- Are we adequately accommodating our more diverse populations? Are we welcoming to, and culturally competent with, people of all backgrounds?

- What is the cost in terms of time and training of becoming and remaining culturally sensitive and competent? What can our peers or state trade associations tell us?

Redefining the family

If you don't think this issue affects you, because you "don't deal with family issues," think again. *Everyone* deals with family issues. Or at least anyone who has a family, or has employees (who have families), or volunteers (who have families), or works for a nonprofit that serves people (who, darn it, also have families).

The changing definition of family is putting stresses and driving changes throughout our society. You need to continue to work to accommodate changing family norms and changing family needs because if you don't, your good staff and volunteers will find a nonprofit that does.

Some questions to discuss with your staff and board:

- What pressures is family change putting on the people we serve? Are we seeing any changes in behavior or needs?

- What about our staff? What percentage of our employees (by generation) are single parents? What can we do to help them? Do we need to review our benefits package to be more accommodating to different situations, such as adoption?

- How do family changes affect our ability to attract and retain volunteers? How can we be sensitive and supportive?

MeBranding

It seems ironic that the generation who bought into the Burger King marketing slogan "Have it your way!" is now a bit overwhelmed by the cacophony of choices, options, combinations, and varieties offered in nearly everything. While MeBranding is not going away unless we move into a major economic collapse, it is such a widespread, nearly ubiquitous phenomenon that it is already spilling over into the way that nonprofits provide services, hire staff, recruit and retain volunteers, and seek donations.

The overall impact of MeBranding will be the assumption of, and demand for, more choices, more customization, more MeServices, more MeBenefits, more MeScheduling, more MeCharity. In reality, this is just the extreme extension of the observation that marketing in nonprofits is about meeting people's needs in a way that they want. And what individuals increasingly want is not to be a *part* of a market, but *to be the market*—one by one.

In a financially stressed world, customization of services, benefits, work environment, and fund development could be very, very challenging. The generational spin on MeBranding? While the demand is higher the younger you are, it is so prevalent culturally that every generation wants it. But, as a nonprofit employee, the older you are the more likely you are to say, "Why should we give every person their own individualized service? People have done *fine* without that before. What a bunch of whiners." And therein lies the trap.

To start, think through these questions.

- In an era of MeServices, how do we get close enough to our customers to know *exactly* what they want?

- What are the financial implications of more customization? The workforce implications?

- Let's look at all of our services and pick two that can be more customized. What would they look like if we MeBrand them?

- What about more flexible benefits and work hours? What does this force us to do, to pay, to become?

- How does this affect our development efforts? What "specialness" can we attach to different kinds of donations?

- How can technology help in any of the "Me" areas?

Work-life balance

While I strongly support people spending less time at work and more at life, I also know that such a trend is not for everyone. The optimal work-life balance is a subjective, moving target, one that changes as career and family changes appear. A young worker who may regularly put in sixty hours a week and then want to hang out with friends may well not feel the same way at age thirty with two small children at home. A desire to be with family may change again when kids leave home for college and leave the nest empty.

In truth, the work-life balance trend is a combination of rebalancing priorities, as well as a bit of MeWork. Particularly for Gen@ and GenX individuals, who saw their parents living to work rather than working to live, work-life balance is a crucial priority, and one employers will have to adjust to.

Here are some starting questions in this area.

- Are we talking to employees and volunteers about their work-life balance? How can our HR function change to deal with this issue?

- What are other employers in our community doing in this area?

- Is our benefits package flexible enough to accommodate different needs of different age employees? What about part-timers (often older) who are entering our workforce?

- How much do we really need our staff at the office? Should we allow work-from-home in some cases? Do we need a policy for that?

- What about work hours, dress code, time off at midday to work out, and so forth? How can we stay in touch with what people want and be helpful without breaking the bank or eroding the team?

Summary

So now you know the brutal facts about the numbers, trends, and impacts your organization must address to remain (or become) a top-caliber non-profit. The facts are as follows:

First, we talked about the definitions and key values of each of the five big generations currently on the scene. These are

1. The Greatest Generation (born 1901–1924)
2. The Silent Generation (born 1925–1945)
3. The Boomers (born 1946–1962)
4. GenX (born 1963–1980)
5. Gen@ (born 1981–2002)

Hopefully, the discussion of each generation's values and characteristics got you, your management team, and board thinking about your current generational diversity and planning.

Next, we looked at six big trends that either result from, or affect, generational change. These are

1. Financial stress
2. Technological acceleration
3. Diversity of population
4. Redefining the family
5. MeBranding
6. Work-life balance

After reviewing these trends we looked at some brief impact ideas, and then a set of questions about each trend to start the discussion at your organization as you begin to examine each trend in more detail.

A final word of advice in the area of trends: Don't take my word for it. So much change is going on around and inside our organizations that the six trends listed may be just the tip of the iceberg for you, or distract you from some other local or trade trends that demand your attention much more. You, your staff, and your board need to have your eyes and ears open to what is happening across the country and around the world. Read widely and think deeply about implications for your workforce, community, and the people your organization serves.

In the next chapter, we'll put the facts in a more specific perspective—how these trends will affect your nonprofit.

3

Generations and Your Organization

THIS CHAPTER LAYS OUT FOUR MAJOR IMPACTS of generations on nonprofits, each of which have many facets for you to consider, plan for, and accommodate.

The good news is that you are no doubt already planning, assessing needs, and looking at market trends. When you do your next Strengths, Weaknesses, Opportunities, and Threats (SWOT) analysis or similar scan, you will need to incorporate generational issues in your planning. And, as we'll see in the remainder of the book, there are staff, board, volunteer, financial, marketing, and technology implications of this change. But in the beginning of this chapter, we'll focus on four overarching impacts:

1. Boomers coming in the door
2. Boomers going out the door
3. Whatever happened to GenX and Gen@?
4. Unintended consequences

Then, we'll look at the meat of the solution. I'll show you Six Big Actions, the techniques that can help you bridge generations, solve generational conflicts, and enhance cross-generation recruitment and retention. You will see these themes throughout every chapter that follows.

By the end of this chapter, you should see some light on the horizon—the dawning of a new day. And a new day of generational issues is fast approaching. So let's get going.

The Four Impacts

Here are the four key impacts that I think will affect your nonprofit in relation to generation change. Each has many facets, but let's go through them one by one. Not surprisingly, just as in day-to-day life, everything revolves around the Boomers.

Boomers coming in the door

This impact has three parts: your staff, the people you serve, and your volunteers.

Staff: Hundreds of thousands of Boomers have done their twenty to twenty-five years in the for-profit/military/government world and, having taken retirement in their first career, are thinking: "Whatever happened to my idealism of the 1960s? I want to do something important." I meet these people all the time when I do training. They come up to me and say: "I loved what you said. I started with my organization a year ago, and with my twenty years in business, I'm still trying to figure out the nonprofit mind-set. . . ." These people are looking for work in the nonprofit sector and have amazing skills. But they haven't yet figured out how to fit in. So how do you find, recruit, and incorporate these people into your staff and volunteer cadre? We'll look at that in our chapter on staff.

Services: If you serve primarily people age sixty years and older, stand back and prepare for the onslaught. Aging services have known this for a long time, but other organizations, such as arts groups, service organizations—anyone with this demographic—need to figure out how they are going to ramp up capacity to serve for ten to twenty years.

> **HANDS ON**: When planning, remember that the Boomers (and all other generational groups) are what are called *age cohorts*. They come and they go, despite Boomers' apparent belief that they'll live forever. Look at the age ranges covered in Chapter 2 and think through the calendar years during which this will affect you. While five or ten years may seem like a long time, it is not in terms of generational trends. The decisions you make now may haunt you in five years.

FOR EXAMPLE: When Boomers were in elementary school, hundreds of school districts built middle schools and high schools to accommodate the coming wave of students. These schools were full for about fifteen years and then half empty for the next twenty. A huge capital expense hung on these districts for a generation. Other districts planned differently, having schools do double shifts, and thus avoided the construction costs and attendant debt. I'm not sure I'd have wanted my kids to go to a split-shift school, but the point is that when dealing with age trends *nothing* is forever.

Volunteers: Finally, millions of Boomers, when they go out the door of their career, have time on their very capable hands. These are people who are often looking to help in their community, *if you give them a cause.* If we're smart, they could be the biggest and best volunteer force in history.

Boomers going out the door

At the same time, people in my generation (Boomers) who have spent their careers in the nonprofit world are deciding on their own retirement plans. Since there have been so many of us, we've clogged up the management/supervision pipeline. Who is going to replace these people? Sheer numbers say we don't have enough skilled managers to fill the slots opening up in the next ten years.

Start in the executive director/CEO seat. Thousands of these people are fifty-five or over and looking longingly at the door. And, in many organizations, the management team, whether large or small, is primarily made up of people of the same Boomer age group. Either willingly, or kicking and screaming, the majority of these people will be gone in ten years.

HANDS ON: Look at your management team. How many are over fifty-five? Do you have a management succession plan? Are you training enough new managers internally?

If you are like most organizations, the answer is no—if for no other reason than you lack a "deep bench." Funders, in their zeal to keep administrative costs down, have severely limited our ability to hire more managers and thus there may be few people to develop. We'll talk more about this in the chapter on staff.

The second twist on Boomers going out the door is centered on your board, and the problem is generally the same. The Boomers make up a huge percentage of boards in the United States, Canada, and the United Kingdom. As they age, they continue to help recruit "themselves," asking people like themselves (read: the same age group) to serve. And the median age of board members rises. Don't believe me? If you have the records, go back ten years and figure the average age of your board then. Then do it for your current board. See? And if your current average age is over fifty-five, do you have a plan for diversifying your board based on age? Why not? We'll talk about this more in Chapter 5.

Whatever happened to GenX and Gen@?

Speaking of volunteers, young people coming out of college have, for at least the past ten years, volunteered more than any generation before them. In fact, the kids coming out of college today probably have volunteered more by graduation than their Boomer parents have in their entire lives. So we are generating a great number of well-trained, experienced, willing volunteers. But, when you look at boards, or groups of volunteers, where are they?

> **FOR EXAMPLE**: I get requests all the time from executive directors and board presidents asking about ways to recruit younger board members and younger volunteers (under thirty). I always answer with this question: "Is everything I would need to know about volunteering, or about serving as a committee member or board member, available online? Everything: meeting times, time obligations, conflict of interest, term of service length, *everything*?" The answer, of course, is almost always "Uh, no." "Then," I say, "they won't come." The reality is that people under thirty are online as comfortably as they breathe. That's where they go for information on everything from movie times to volunteering opportunities at your organization.

HANDS ON: Do you have the ability to accept donations online with credit cards and PayPal? Do you have *complete* information about available volunteering, board service, and other opportunities on your web site, including ways to send you follow-up questions by e-mail? You need to. Words to recruit by: If you build it—they may not show up. If you build it *online*—they just might.

We need to have active programs to recruit younger volunteers. Again, this is simple demographics—our Greatest Generation volunteers are dying out, our Boomer volunteers are finishing careers and will retire. If we don't fill the pipeline with younger volunteers, we won't have much to choose from in five to ten years.

Unintended consequences

The law of unintended consequences is pervasive. For example, the United Way of America reacted to its scandals in the early 1990s by offering donors the option to target their donations to particular organizations. This action was intended to make donors more comfortable with the United Way, but no one really expected the number of donors who chose that option. The result was less money for United Way community groups to distribute. In another case, the City of Chicago decided that its high-rise, low-income apartments were a failure, and, over the past ten years, has been tearing them down, redistributing the residents all over the city. Unexpected result? The failure of many nonprofits located by the former high-rise sites, dedicated to helping residents. By moving residents away from support sources, the ability to help them went down.

In complex social systems, we can't foresee everything that may happen, or predict with certainty human behavior. So, here are some unintended consequences to mull over:

- What will Boomers do in their retirement? First, will they retire at sixty or seventy or ever? If they don't retire "on schedule" what will the effect be on GenX staff?

- In retirement, will Boomer volunteer hours go up, go down, or stay the same?

- What about donations? Will Boomers be economically stressed in retirement and not make their regular donations, or will they keep the flow of money coming?

- What about GenX and Gen@ perspectives as they move into management positions at our funders? What will they think about our traditional service array?

- How will the new, younger cohorts—many of whom have academic degrees in nonprofit management but little direct experience—manage? Will a professional-management class have the level of mission passion that nonprofits have been built on? Will these managers retain a willingness to sacrifice some financial and career benefits for a cause?

These "big four" impacts will be with us for the next fifteen to twenty years. We need to be aware of the main issues and, as the final impact indicates, stay flexible as unexpected consequences arise. In the meantime, let's focus on what we can do *right now:* Six Big Actions to deal with generational change.

Six Big Actions

While there are many things you might do to prepare for the change upon us, six stand out. I call them the "Six Big Actions" because taking them will smooth your ride through the coming transition. (In the rest of this book, you'll see these items over and over as we put them into action.) Here they are:

- Include generational issues in planning
- Mentor and discuss among generations
- Target market by generation
- Age down
- Meet techspectations
- Ask

These six big actions (and their many spin-off actions) will form the core of the remainder of the book. We'll look at them in relation to staff, board, the people you serve, marketing, technology, and finance. Right now, though, let's examine each in a bit more detail and in a generic fashion.

Include generational issues in planning

If you don't already have strategic, marketing, and financial plans, generational preparedness is a great reason to get them in place. While generation change is not an immediate crisis, it certainly will become one without adequate preparation. So, you must incorporate generational change into your planning at all levels, sooner rather than later.

> **FOR EXAMPLE**: A nonprofit client of mine recently decided to add generational change as a component of its plans. This organization provides meals, housing, and transportation to ex-offenders, as well as some job support for parolees. Its annual budget is about $3.3 million, and in a good year it breaks even. It does some direct fundraising, but most of its income comes from government and foundations interested in post-incarceration issues.
>
> The agency did a generational assessment, and found that while the average age of its service recipients had been steady for ten years at between twenty-five and twenty-nine, the average age of its staff has risen to forty-four, and its board's mean age was fifty-six. The management team (four people) had an average tenure of twenty-three years, an average age of fifty-seven, and only their Social Security and whatever they'd been able to save in their personal IRAs to count on in retirement. Thus, when interviewed, management felt they could not afford to retire in the foreseeable future. One area where the organization felt good was in intergenerational staff conflict. Very little of that occurred because a key part of the organizational service array focused on mentoring, which took place both inside the agency (between staff) and outside (from staff to clients).

The board and staff concluded that they needed three things: First, a younger board to stay closer to the age of their key service recipients; second, a leadership development and succession plan for their staff; and third, contributions to the retirement funds of employees with more than five years of service, with a temporarily higher rate of contribution for employees who were both over fifty and had worked for the agency for more than fifteen years.

These goals affected the entire agency. Many, many questions had to be addressed. If the organization was just breaking even financially, where would it get the money for retirement contributions or for leadership development? What about the current board members? How would they feel about moving over for younger members? Would younger staff stay long enough to see their career paths open up with the retirement of long-term management? What effect would the aging of the community in general have on the demand for the agency's services? On its governmental funding?

The board and staff agreed to a major revision of their strategic plan, including a focus on its long-term financial situation. This activity, which took nearly a year, revitalized the staff, set specific goals in their three key areas of concern, and brought the issue of generational change front and center for both staff and board.

HANDS ON: As you read this book, make a baseline assessment of your situation in relation to generations. The Generational Self-Assessment worksheet at the end of this chapter (page 52) is designed to help you do exactly that. As you work through each chapter, come back to the assessment and fill in the areas that you have just covered in your reading. Your responses will give you a baseline for discussion and planning. As with the agency in the example above, you may be fine in some areas, while in others you may see a looming crisis.

Then, make sure that you add generational issues to your planning from now on, whether it be in marketing, finance, service provision, human resources, or overall strategic planning.

Mentor and discuss among generations

Mentoring and open discussion are crucial in solving intergenerational conflict. You need to set up both formal and informal mentoring and discussions to break down barriers between generations. Whether with staff or in your volunteer cadre, mentoring passes on *knowledge and perspective,* both of which are crucial. A young person might well wonder why a Greatest Generation grandparent is so frugal (stingy? cheap?), and could look at them negatively. But when they talk to that grandparent and hear their stories of living through the Great Depression, the grandparent's perspective becomes much clearer.

As a leader and supervisor this requires your constant attention, preventive action, and quick response if and when conflict arises. Admittedly, not all interpersonal conflict is based on generational issues (just as it is not always based on race, income, nationality, or high school of origin), but if you aren't looking for generational conflict at all, you'll never diagnose it.

Some of these discussions can be formal, but also try to facilitate more informal discussions, lunches, coffees, roundtables, and get-to-know-you sessions that will open some doors. In terms of more formal mentoring, remember that it should NOT always occur using *older* mentors and *younger* mentees.

> **FOR EXAMPLE**: One of my absolute favorite mentoring stories is about Jack Welch when he was CEO of General Electric. In 1991, Welch and a friend of his were attending a business roundtable meeting. After the meeting, the friend asked Welch if he had time to have lunch. Welch deferred, saying that he had to hurry back to his office for a meeting with his mentor.
>
> "Your *what*? You don't mean *your* mentor. . . . You're mentoring someone? Who?" said the friend.
>
> "No, I have a mentor," said Welch, "and he's twenty-four."
>
> "No way," said the friend. Then Welch told the story.
>
> About a year earlier Welch had walked by a workstation where a young employee was working. The screen looked different than anything Welch

had seen, so he asked the employee what he was doing. The youngster told Welch he was looking at GE's competition's sales and marketing information. "How did you get it?" asked Welch. The youngster shrugged and said, "It's all online, Mr. Welch. You just gotta go look."

Welch asked the employee to come to his office the next day. Remember, this was in 1990, and it was not clear that the Internet was going to be much more than a geek thing. But there was a new piece of software called Mozilla, later Netscape, that made access to the Internet much, much easier. The young man came to Welch's office and spent two hours explaining how the Internet and networking could help GE. Welch immediately assigned him as Welch's tech mentor, and they spent two hours together each week for a year. At the same time, Welch mandated that all of GE's top managers find their own technology mentor, and that the mentor be under thirty years of age.

The result? GE was far, far ahead of its competition with online sales, service, parts, marketing, and its own intranet.

The GenX and Gen@ employees and volunteers at your organization have lots to tell you, so don't prejudice the discussion by assuming that older is always more learned.

HANDS ON: The best place to start here is with yourself. Pick out an employee or volunteer of a different generation and have coffee, breakfast, or lunch. Talk to them about their perspective on the organization, what they see as the biggest needs, the best things, the worst things, and so on. Listen much more than you talk, take notes, and then do it again with someone from yet another generation. Start to notice the different responses and attitudes.

Once you've done this for a while with a number of staff and volunteers, get together three focus groups . . . one of Gen@, one GenX, and one of Boomers. Find a facilitator for the discussion for each group from the same generation. Have each facilitator ask the same questions:

- At our agency, is it hard or easy to relate to older (younger) employees and volunteers? Why?

- What have you learned recently from older (younger) workers or volunteers? How did you learn it?

- What bugs you most about people of a different age group?

- What do you value most about working at our agency? What one thing would you change to improve things?

- Where do you see yourself in ten years?

With a group of ten to fifteen people, these questions will easily fill up ninety minutes. You'll be amazed at the differences in the answers.

Use this effort to start more intergenerational discussions, and work toward mentoring, which we'll look at more in Chapter 4, Generations and Staff.

Target market by generation

As you will see in Chapter 7, Marketing to Generations, rethinking your marketing efforts by generation is crucial to dealing effectively with generational change. While the traditional marketing process is the same, the emphasis and sensitivity analysis is significantly different.

FOR EXAMPLE: Gen@ simply isn't interested in what Boomers consider traditional marketing and advertising venues. "The network evening news? What's that? I get my news on Google, or learn about stuff from blogs, or from *The Daily Show*. . . . Newspaper? Yeah, I read the *New York Times* online. . . ."

Even within traditional advertisement, look at the Boomer-centric emphasis—just count the gray hairs on the advertising actors, look at the ads for retirement communities, or as a friend of mine said recently: "Dear me, we've gone from ads about Pampers to ads about Depends in about ten years." Madison Avenue gets this. Do we in our organizations?

FOR EXAMPLE: Recently I was doing a presentation on generation change to a room full of executives. I noted that having more and more material online is crucial—it's what the market wants. I provided them a long list of things that donors wanted, and one exec grumpily put his hand up and said, "Why should we put all those things right online and make it so easy? Donors should be willing to do a little work. Young people are just getting lazy."

My view? He's toast.

In the chapter on marketing I'll give you some tools to assess by generation. This is actually just a slightly different lens than the one you've been using to date, but it's really important as Boomers move through, move on, and are backfilled by GenX and Gen@.

Age down

This is both the simplest and most difficult action to take. It is simple, in that you compute the mean age for your board, management, volunteers, and donors, and actively seek to reduce that age. It is very difficult in that you must balance your efforts to reduce the mean age against the principle of nondiscrimination and the huge value of Boomers and Greatest Generation members to your organization. But in general, you want to seek to lower the mean age of your organization's core constituency.

And here's the secret. You can plan this, or it *will* just happen helter-skelter. The Boomers *are* turning sixty. They *will* turn sixty-five, then seventy. They *will* retire and die. But if you wait for the natural occurrence of things, you'll be behind the curve.

Let me be clear. When I say "age down," I am not advocating age discrimination. You can't fire people, or reject job applicants, based on their age. Age discrimination is flat-out illegal, and you should not even think about going there. But you can think about aging down in other nondiscriminatory ways.

> **HANDS ON**: Here are three things you can do to age down in your organization.
>
> • Seek to recruit younger board members, people in their midtwenties to midthirties. Include generation thinking in your skill set for board recruitment.

- Seek more college-age and twenty-something volunteers.

- Start a leadership development program with your youngest managers and staff members. This program should have the goals of current improvement and longer-term retention of your best young workers.

As you age down you will meet the rising tide of the next generations directly, incorporate them into the mainstream of your organization, and prepare the organization to move beyond its current fixation on Boomers.

There are other benefits as well, and we'll discuss them in a lot more detail in the chapter on Generations on Staff.

Meet techspectations

Technology is so important to your mission effectiveness, organizational development, marketing, fundraising, and management that it is essentially ubiquitous as we think of our organizations. The problem with the word "ubiquitous" is that it often morphs into "invisible," which means we don't think about it enough.

Well, as we deal with generation change, we need to actively deal with technology. First, the obvious: Gen@. Their techspectations, as staff, as board, as funders, as users of our services, will be higher and less forgiving than any other in history. GenX is not far behind.

For Boomers? Well, Boomer workers coming in from the private sector in a second career will have high techspectations. Additionally, they are likely to have greater accessibility requirements because of hearing, vision, and motor problems.

> **FOR EXAMPLE**: A cell-phone company is responding to the aging market with simpler cell phones. These phones will not have e-mail, cameras, or web access. They will have larger screens, both visual and auditory cues to remind you that you have messages and that your battery is running down, and bigger keys. That is smart, generation-specific marketing.

The key here is to look at ways to use technology to bridge the generation divide, to accommodate the wants of different age groups, to make your organization more efficient and effective as it goes through generational change. (Thus Chapter 8 on technology and generations.)

Different generations have different techspectations, to be sure. But, as with so much else in organizational development, not everyone fits into a nice predictable stereotype. Thus it is imperative that in performing this activity, you add to it the next one: asking.

Ask

The last Big Action: Ask.

Whenever you cross into new territory, it is smart to ask, observe, and listen. When you go to a new country you do that. When you go into a new neighborhood you do that. When you start at a new school, or in a new job, you do that. But in each of these cases you know you are on new ground because it is physically under your feet.

With generational issues, we are often on new turf as well, but we just don't realize it. We need to be asking, and asking constantly. Our past experience may be helpful, but there is so much to learn in this new area. I've been studying the issue of generational conflict, generational impact for a couple of years now, and I've talked to hundreds of people about it. But I still learn something significant nearly *every* time I ask a new person about the issue. And, frankly, I learn more significant stuff talking to people from GenX or Gen@ than the Boomers. Why? Because I *am* a Boomer; that's *my* turf.

Often what I observe (and interpret) is different than what I hear. This is a danger to any of us—we interpret through our own generational lenses. If we don't ask and listen, we risk misinterpreting intentions and increasing conflict.

FOR EXAMPLE: Here's a very, very common source of conflict.

Boomer manager to Gen@ worker: "I need you to come in this weekend. We've got some work that needs to be done."

Gen@ worker: "Oh, sorry, I'd love to help, but I have a family obligation this weekend."

Boomer: "Well, I'm sorry, but this has to be done. I'll be here all weekend, and I'd appreciate a little help."

Gen@: "OK, well, I can't come in, but I'll get it done during the week next week. That way I can make the family thing and still help out. How's that?"

Boomer (grumpily as he walks away): "I guess that will have to do."

Boomer thinks: *The guy has no commitment to us. He just doesn't care.*

Gen@ thinks: *The guy needs a life.*

And both are frustrated. But if the manager was more aware of Gen@'s motivation (work to live) and if Gen@ was more aware of the Boomer's motivation (live to work), while they still might not agree, they would understand more about the other, and hopefully be a bit more forgiving.

HANDS ON: In everything, whether it is mentoring and discussing, or marketing to target generations, or even trying to meet techspectations, ask, ask, ask—and listen. And remember, the first three (the asking) is much, much easier than the listening.

You will see suggestions on asking throughout the remainder of this book.

Now you know the Big Six Actions that you will see throughout the remainder of the book. You'll have plenty of opportunity to use them as we move forward from here. But where is "here" for your organization? What's your current situation related to generational change? Would you like to get a feeling for what your organizational readiness is? Good! That's the subject of the next section.

Generational Self-Assessment

If you want to measure your success as you bring generations into your planning, you need a starting point. This section will help you figure out where you're at now. You can revisit it annually to check progress. You can mark this assessment in this book, or take it online at the publisher's web site. Go to www.FieldstoneAlliance.org and search "Generational Self-Assessment."

This assessment is designed to get you thinking about where your organization is in relation to the effect generational change will have on your services, your staff, your volunteers, and your technology.

Unlike many assessments, this one is not scored. Rather, it is designed to get you started looking at the facts for your organization. There are many, many **HANDS ON** ideas throughout the book, and questions at the end of each chapter that will help you think through what you need to do. But the first job is to figure out where you are.

Part A: Internal Generational Status

In this section, fill in the numbers and percentages of people fitting into each generational group. Start with the raw numbers. The columns include both the generation name and the birth years for that generation. If you don't have actual data (particularly for service recipients), estimate as best as you can. Once you have entered the numbers and totaled them, divide each number by the total for that line. The result is the percentage. For example, if the employee total is 41, and the Gen@ number of employees is 8, the percentage is 8/41 or 19.5 percent. If you total your percentages, they should sum to 100 percent (plus or minus your rounding errors). Note that in areas where you may have "part" of a person (as in the person is part time) you should still count that person as one. Let's say your official count shows you as having 10.5 FTEs (full-time equivalents), which includes 3 who work half-time. You would actually count 12 employees—9 full-time staff plus 3 part-time staff. Once you have done the entry and calculations for board, volunteers, and employees, compare that to the community. You can get your community data from the U.S. Census web site, www.census.gov. How do your percentages compare to those of your community?

Board, Volunteers, Employees, and Community by Generation

		Gen@ 1981–2002	GenX 1963–1980	Boomers 1946–1962	Silent 1925–1945	Greatest 1901–1924	Total
Board	#						
	%						100%
Volunteers	#						
	%						100%
Employees	#						
	%						100%
Community	#						
	%						100%

Part B: Generational Services Status

Now let's examine your services. The table on page 54 is set up the same as the one above, except that the left-hand column is blank: you need to fill in the services one by one. If you have more services than available rows, copy the table and fill out as many as you need. *Note:* To be sure that you include it, I have filled in one row: individual donors. While donors are not necessarily service recipients, you need to take a look at them by generation as well.

Service Recipients by Generation

Service area		Gen@ 1981–2002	GenX 1963–1980	Boomers 1946–1962	Silent 1925–1945	Greatest 1901–1924	Total
	#						
	%						100%
	#						
	%						100%
	#						
	%						100%
	#						
	%						100%
	#						
	%						100%
	#						
	%						100%
	#						
	%						100%
	#						
	%						100%
	#						
	%						100%
Donors	#						
	%						100%

After finishing this chart, get your staff together and talk about your generational focus. Which services are skewed younger, which older? Which services do you depend on financially, or in terms of community perception?

Summary

In this chapter, you've learned more about how generational change affects your nonprofit directly. First, we looked at four key impacts on your organization, with relevant examples and some questions. The Four Impacts are

1. Boomers coming in the door

2. Boomers going out the door

3. Whatever happened to GenX and Gen@?

4. Unintended consequences

Next we looked at Six Big Actions to deal with generation change in your organization. Whether working with staff, marketing to end-users, or recruiting volunteers, these techniques will help you move your organization through the generational change that is upon us.

These Six Big Actions are

- Include generational issues in planning

- Mentor and discuss among generations

- Target market by generation

- Age down

- Meet techspectations

- Ask

You'll see these six actions repeatedly throughout the remainder of the book. They will form the core of your plans as you look at generational change.

Finally, you completed a generational assessment to get a baseline for your organization's generational profile as you begin this work. Save that assessment, as you'll want to revisit it in future years.

So, now you know the preliminary things needed to get the most out of the implementation part of this book. In Part Two, we'll examine impacts and remedies for staff, board, and volunteers, the people you serve, marketing, technology, and finance. Enough preparation. Let's get to the implementation!

PART TWO

Where We're Going

I'm sixty and would like to retire in a couple of years, but there is no one here who I'm comfortable passing the job to, and we've never had (or been allowed to have) enough administrative depth to accommodate a succession plan. I don't want to leave the organization high and dry. What are my options?

I worry that our board is getting so old. We need younger board members—quickly—or there will be no tomorrow for us.

Tech, tech, tech. I'm so sick of this tech stuff. We have too much emphasis on this, and not enough on people.

We are so tech deficient, I can't believe it. No one can find us, our web site is terrible, none of our documents are online. We're so inefficient it makes my head hurt.

4

Generations on Staff

YOUR ORGANIZATION NEEDS YOUR GOOD STAFF more than your good staff need your organization. A good staff comes in a variety of shapes, sizes, backgrounds, and ages. In this, the first of six implementation chapters, we'll explore the issue of generations on your staff and how to best implement a generation strategy that accounts for, values, recruits, and retains the best people from all the different generations.

We'll first look at the Four Impacts and how they relate to your staff. This is followed by two employee-related issues that are vexing many organizations: executive transition and work-life balance. These issues are crucial for your next five to ten years. Finally, we'll see how the Six Big Actions relate to your employees, with some long-range considerations as well as a checklist for immediate implementation.

By the end of this chapter, you'll have a much better handle on how to wrestle with generational issues on your staff.

The Four Impacts and Your Staff

The Four Impacts are Boomers coming in the door, Boomers going out the door, whatever happened to GenX and Gen@?, and unintended consequences. Let's see how they'll affect your staff.

Boomers coming in the door

This impact is already here, and it is only going to grow. Boomers coming in the door are coming to you from two directions, and for two reasons. First, the directions: the Boomer who has retired specifically to start a second career with a nonprofit, and the Boomer who has retired on schedule but has decided to return to work.

FOR EXAMPLE: John, a fifty-four-year-old marketing executive, has had a great run at his company, but has worried recently about whether he is really "making a difference." He remembers his time of social activism in college, and of helping the poor during a postcollege stint in VISTA in New Mexico. His oldest child has just graduated from college, and John and his wife agree that he needs a change. He does not want to volunteer: he sees volunteers as "old guys pushing people around in wheelchairs in hospitals." He feels his marketing skills could be of great value for many nonprofits. And he likes working. John knows he will take a salary cut, but that's fine with him. He retires, takes his company pension, and begins to look for a place to work at one of the many nonprofits in his community.

After a three-month search, he takes a interesting position with the local wilderness protection organization. John's job is to let the public know more about the value of even small sections of preserved wilderness, and to integrate the idea of land donation into the community's more traditional fundraising habits.

Culture clashes begin from day one. John wants to use his full marketing experience and expertise while his boss, Matt, a dedicated wilderness activist, just wants John to "sell the mission." John notes that the organization has been losing ground in fundraising, and thinks they should reevaluate what the public wants from the organization. Evaluation metrics should be kept, and the organization should be more accountable to the public. Matt's answer? "We *know* what we need. We don't need to ask . . . just go sell. We don't have the money to evaluate, we've got to spend every dime we do have on acquiring new land."

How long do you think this relationship will last?

John's and Matt's different perspectives are typical of the conflict that arises when Boomers come in the door after years of working in a different sector or different organizational culture. Understand more than anything: Boomers want to work, and Boomers *want a cause*. In our organizations, we can offer both, but we shouldn't expect someone with twenty or thirty years of experience to just toss away that knowledge and instantly do things our way. Beside, we are *hiring them for their expertise*. Why then do we so often ignore it and expect people with vast expertise to simply adopt our methods? Worse, why do we hire people whose skills require resources we don't have, or conditions we don't face? It always seems to me like buying a four-wheel drive vehicle to use solely in a sun-belt city. What's the point?

> **HANDS ON**: When you think about hiring Boomers—particularly if they are going to join the top management ranks—have extended discussions about their duties, your resources, your expectations, and their expectations. If they have not yet left their long-term employer, think about having the Boomer take some vacation time and work with you for a week or two to get a better handle on your culture. Make sure they interview with most, if not all, of the management team. Assign them a mentor, and be prepared to check in with them more than you would other employees for the first few months. And remember, give them a cause!

Now, the reasons Boomers come in the door: they come because they want to make a contribution to the community and because they need something—a salary, or benefits, or both. In the best-case scenario, you can combine these two reasons to give people a valuable, long-term employment opportunity.

> **FOR EXAMPLE**: Mitch[3] had retired after thirty years driving a long-distance eighteen-wheeler. He had a medical condition that was causing problems when driving at night. His former employer, in financial distress, cut pension benefits (particularly health care) for current and former workers, so Mitch found himself needing some extra income and a better health care package. Active in his church, Mitch was often involved in outreach into the community, where he came in contact with the executive director of the local BigHeart nonprofit. BigHeart

---

[3] This story is true, but names of people and organizations have been altered.

helps the community by selling used goods and passing on the profits to people in need. BigHeart was having trouble keeping drivers for the trucks they used to haul donated goods from store to store and throughout the region. BigHeart's executive director suggested that Mitch come and drive for BigHeart, and Mitch agreed, but only if he could work limited hours, and only if he was eligible for health care coverage. The executive director and the management team met to discuss this aberration from normal part-time benefits, and decided that Mitch was too good to pass up.

Mitch signed on to drive ten hours a week, and became enamored of the people with disabilities he met at BigHeart's stores and other places of employment. Within his first four months at BigHeart, Mitch encouraged two of his former driving buddies (who had also retired) to come to BigHeart. They formed a core of highly experienced drivers who were dependable and accident free. One additional benefit: because of their driving record and license level, BigHeart's insurance premiums on their trucks went down.

HANDS ON: Remember the sixth Big Action, Ask? How about the third, Target market by generation? Both actions apply here. When Boomers come in the door (or if you invite them in by recruiting them), don't just look at their skills. . . . *ask* about their motivations. In the case above, BigHeart was flexible—and even decided to rewrite its rules—to hire a highly skilled employee with special needs.

Boomers coming in the door present flexibility and perspective challenges, but they also offer a significant array of skills, experience, and maturity.

Caution: Remember, if you are a Boomer executive director, and your management team is all Boomers, and you are hiring all part-time Boomers, you are probably doing two things: staying in your comfort zone (hiring people you understand) and aging up, not down, which is contrary to Big Action number 4. So be careful.

Boomers going out the door

What happens when a management team of all Boomers leaves within a five-year stretch? Tick, tick, tick . . . this time bomb is absolutely going to go off at countless nonprofits over the next decade. The Annie E. Casey Foundation's 2004 Nonprofit Executive Leadership and Transitions Survey found that Boomers now comprise over *72 percent* of nonprofit leadership—with 55 percent over the age of fifty. That's our *rock*. Our funders and watchdogs have given us our *hard place* in the form of flattened administrative functions that leave no room for adequate management positions where people can learn the job of an executive director, deputy director, or other key roles.

So, if you are a typical nonprofit in relation to the Casey study, three out of four of your senior managers will probably be eyeing retirement—if they can afford it.

This has other, perhaps unexpected, downsides. First, a lot of Boomers don't want to go out the door. They are very, very afraid of what's on the other side.

> **HANDS ON**: Look at the ages of your senior managers (you may already have done this in the Generational Self-Assessment) and start to talk to these people openly about your retirement plans as a way of getting them to talk about theirs. This is not always easy, or simple.

> **FOR EXAMPLE**: Joe Paterno, the extremely successful and very long-time coach of the Penn State Nittany Lions Football team was asked to do an advertisement for a senior retirement community a few years ago. Paterno (as of this writing) has never mentioned even the thought of retirement publicly. According to stories on ESPN, the television ad for the retirement community had to be rewritten several times so that Paterno didn't have to use the word "retire"—he had tremendous trouble simply saying the word.

While Paterno is no Boomer (he is a member of the Silent Generation), his problem in confronting the word "retirement" certainly is one that many

Boomers in nonprofits share. We talk about retirement, even plan for it, but when it rears its head we often blanch. What will we do? How will we identify ourselves if not through our work? What value will we have to the community, to ourselves? After all, we've *already been part of the nonprofit world*. We can't go make a life change like Mitch and start working for a nonprofit!

Second, if there is widespread expectation that retirement occurs at age sixty-two or sixty-five, the GenX people who have been waiting for the Boomers to gracefully leave (or get out of the way, depending on their level of frustration) may be unhappily surprised if their Boomer managers start talking about not leaving until they are seventy, or "dying with my boots on." This is a sensitive issue—on lots of levels. We'll talk about it a bit more later, but always handle it with care.

> **HANDS ON**: Get going on a transition plan for your Boomers. Look for help in the Resources section of this book. This may well be a ten-year plan, but it has lots of components, including leadership development, financial planning, establishment and growth of retirement funds, education of both board and staff on the issues surrounding transition, and a long-term focus to help the organization make the optimal smooth generational transition.

One more thing about Boomers going out the door: remember that it isn't just managers who are leaving. It's good, hard-working, long-tenured people from *all* levels of the organization. So, while we naturally focus most on the management team, you need to look at your organization's entire staff as well.

Whatever happened to GenX and Gen@?

We lack GenX and Gen@ members on our boards and in our volunteer cadres, even though these generations started volunteering earlier than generations before them. But what about these two generations on staff? Are they showing up? Are they staying? Are they having the career satisfaction they want and deserve?

FOR EXAMPLE: I do a fair bit of informal career counseling for my graduate students at Northwestern University's Kellogg School of Management. As a real-world practitioner rather than a full-time academic, they see me as a conduit and sounding board regarding jobs in the charitable sector. After graduation, I manage to keep in touch with a few students from each class, checking in with them about their work.

The students are mostly Gen@ with a few GenXers sprinkled in. All of them are blindingly smart, incredibly successful young people. A vast majority who take my class either have worked in one or more nonprofits or have served on charitable boards of directors. So they are smart, willing, and experienced. Here is a sampling of things they have told me over the last few years.

"The organizations that I have looked at are paying a lot less than the private sector, which I expected. But on top of that, they have hardly any benefits, no retirement, a crappy health care plan. I have a husband and two kids. I want to work in the sector, but I don't see being able to afford it."

"Two places I interviewed were pretty much the same: both wanted me to come on as CFO, and 'clean up Dodge City.' It seemed to me that what they wanted was a hammer, since the CEO, who had been there ten years or so, had let things go. In both places, the CEO was a visionary, very personable, but not very organized. And in both places the CEO was in his or her early fifties. I realized that I would come in as CFO and either clean the place up and then leave, or be CFO until I was fifty. There was no upward mobility."

"After college, I went into the Peace Corps, and then did a year for an NGO in Central America. Now that I have this wonderful and wickedly expensive MBA, I want to use it in the charitable sector, but my student loans are killer. I have to work in the for-profit world for a few years and then hopefully return to the nonprofit sector. I can't make enough in the nonprofit world to both make my loan payments and eat."

"I want to work in the nonprofit world, and plan to for a few years. But I worked at a nonprofit in college and did pro bono consulting for a couple of others when I worked for a (Big Five) consulting firm, and I gotta tell you, their passion is great, but those people do not have lives beyond work. I want to have kids and actually see them grow up. So, I'll work for a nonprofit for a few years and then move back to the for-profit world, where things are a little saner."

As of this writing, two of the four students quoted above are not working in the nonprofit sector, and the third plans to leave their current nonprofit position within a year. Only one is looking to stay longer term in the sector.

So, what do we do to recruit and retain the GenX and Gen@ worker? First, we recognize that their motivations are different, their desires are different, and then, after we put them all in a nice generational box, we ask them about their motivations and desires, because not everyone fits into a nice generational box. Remember that your employees are individuals who each come from a lot of backgrounds: their family, the community where they grew up, their education, their ethnicity, their personal experience, and, of course, their generation. Each of us has all those pieces of background packed into the baggage we lug with us through life.

So, ask, listen *with generational sensitivity,* and then accommodate as you can, just as you would with any other market.

HANDS ON: As part of your transition planning, examine *with your employees* your recruitment, retention, continuing education, benefits, employee handbook, and everything else that has to do with your employees. If the majority of your midlevel staff are in their thirties with young families, do you accommodate their time needs well from their perspective? Have you included them in your review of benefits, or is only the senior management team (who are probably mostly Boomers) doing the review?

If you are attempting to increase communication across generational lines, this is a great place to start.

Of course, despite your best recruitment and retention efforts, Gen@ and GenX staff will leave. Losing staff is inevitable. They leave for all kinds of reasons, but after they leave they have a unique perspective on the organization, its strengths, and weaknesses.

> **HANDS ON**: Have a process by which an *independent third party* contacts your former employees three months and again one year after they leave and asks them questions such as: How do you feel about your time at the organization? What can the organization do to make the employment experience a better one? What were the best and worst things about working there? Would you recommend working there to your friends? Why or why not? You want to do this for any former employee—but then break out the answers by program (in case there is a supervision issue) and then by generation, to see if there are generational improvements you can make.

Hopefully, with some work, we can significantly reduce the impact of losing GenX and Gen@ employees in the next ten years. Then, when we look at our employees (and our volunteers, whom we'll deal with in the next chapter) we'll say, "Whatever happened to GenX and Gen@? Look! They're right here!" Because if we can't say that, if we aren't successful in GenX and Gen@ recruitment and retention—who *will* be there? A bunch of *really* old Boomers, that's who.

Unintended consequences

Big change brings about unintended consequences, some good, some not so good. With generation change, we'll have some surprises as well, but the more we are prepared for the predictable stuff, the more flexibility we'll have to adapt to the unexpected.

Unintended consequences show up with the people we serve, with our board, and with our employees. We are, after all, people. And, we do weird, wonderful, and often totally unanticipated things.

FOR EXAMPLE: One of my favorite stories about employees behaving in ways that were not intended at all has to do with my father-in-law, Luke. Luke, at the time this story took place, was about to turn sixty and was an executive in charge of general agents at a large insurance firm. A career man, Luke was loyal, hard-working, and good at his job. He returned home on a Friday afternoon from a long road trip to find a note from his secretary saying he absolutely had to come to work before close of business that day. Luke called the secretary, asking what the big crisis was. She told him in no uncertain terms that he "wanted to come in and see something."

So, he put his tie back on and went to the office to find that he, like over one hundred senior execs with the firm, had been offered an early retirement package. Up to that moment, Luke and his wife had hoped to be able to figure out a way to retire when Luke turned sixty-three, but they were resigned to his working to age sixty-five. Luke took the paperwork home, ran the numbers, and found out that the package was so good that he could retire in less than six months. He came in on Monday, walked into his boss's office, and laid his letter of retirement on the boss's desk. The boss protested: "Luke, we didn't mean you! We just wanted to move aside some of our 'deadwood' to make room for younger managers. But we don't want you to leave! Please reconsider!" My recollection of the rest of the story is that, of the one hundred or so execs who got the offer, 90 percent, like Luke, took the money and ran. The firm's top management, who lived to work, never thought through what they were offering *from the perspective of the managers they wanted to keep.*

Top management's ignorance of their staff's perspectives (a failure to ask) had major unintended consequences for the organization. Besides losing many valuable staff members, a number of younger managers needed to be promoted *before they were ready for larger jobs.* Five years later the organization was in serious financial trouble. A tougher economy and other factors also helped its decline, but the lack of management readiness for a big transition hurt them.

What unintended consequences can we anticipate? Two have popped up in the past year, one related to academic training of new managers and the other related to transition plans.

When I began my consulting career in 1982, there were two university-based programs in nonprofit management, at Case Western and Yale. Today there are hundreds of undergraduate and graduate programs for nonprofit managers at universities across North America, Europe, and Asia. These offer a much higher level of educational opportunity than ever for nonprofit professionals, with a wonderful spin-off benefit of good, solid research in the field for the first time.

As these highly educated new managers come out of undergrad and grad school, they go directly into the middle and senior management ranks of nonprofits *without ever having worked at the line of service*. And therein lies the unintended consequence. Prior generations of nonprofit managers learned their management skills on the job. Not necessarily the best method, but they had no choice. Because of this line experience these older managers earned "street cred" with their line staff. The managers had themselves done what the line workers were doing. But the new, highly trained managers often don't have that or, if they do, their line experience has been at another kind of agency or another nonprofit discipline altogether—and creds don't travel well. Thus, the resentment builds from both directions: The in-place managers don't think the new ones have a clue, and the new, highly educated managers feel that the existing managers are out of date and using old methods.

HANDS ON: This is a problem we can solve. The hospital industry in the 1970s had the same issue and overcame it. When you hire one or more of these highly educated and prepared graduates, you need to communicate and mentor. Immediately upon arrival, talk to the new hire about the need for understanding the passion of the organization where the mission is provided, and then assign the new manager a *line staff* mentor who will educate the new hire to the realities of the "street" where you work. This will do two things: open lines of communication, and make the new person accessible and real to the line staff member and all of their peers. Make sure that the mentor also has enough tenure to talk about the history of the organization, its traditions, and its challenges.

A second unintended consequence grows from the rapid establishment of transition plans. Contrary to retaining GenXers, these have in some cases accelerated their departure. Why? GenX staffers assumed that their bosses would be leaving at sixty or sixty-five—or at least *soon*. But when the plan is done and the bosses for the first time acknowledge that they either have no plans to leave, or plan to leave only if they die, staffers face the new information squarely and move on.

> **HANDS ON**: Don't let this kind of information get out ahead of you. Make sure that the first interviews with the senior staff, in which they say things such as "Huh. I really don't have any plans to retire," or "I'd love to work until I'm seventy-five!" (but are speaking off the cuff and without long consideration), don't work their way through the rumor mill and become "She's NEVER LEAVING!" and precipitate unnecessary stress or worse, departures of valuable staff. In many cases I've seen, the desired date of departure for the executive is far, far later than the board thinks is wise. Make sure that the staff have all the information before they take the rumor and run.

Those are the Four Impacts from the employee perspective. But two other issues—executive transitions and work-life balance—require more depth.

Executive transitions

Earlier in this chapter I noted that the Annie E. Casey Foundation's 2004 Nonprofit Executive Leadership and Transitions Survey found that Boomers now comprise over 72 percent of nonprofit leadership—with 55 percent over the age of fifty. That's enough of a challenge, but it's worse than that. The foundation also asked current executives how long they planned to stay in their position and found that 65 percent expected to be in their position only *five years or less!* Finally, the foundation study also established that more than a third of executives either helped found their organizations, or have been in their job more than ten years, or both. Thus, the organization may have never "known" leadership other than in the person who is currently filling the seat.

Here's a process to get you on the road to dealing with this situation.

1. **Assess the situation.** The Generational Self-Assessment in Chapter 3 offers some help in this area. Basically, you want to examine your risk of a *planned* succession in the executive director's chair over the next five to ten years. Obviously, the first place to start is with the executive. How old is she? How many years has she been the executive? What are her plans about retirement, if any? How deep is your management "bench"? Do you have a leadership development program already?

2. **Develop a contingency plan.** Sometimes planned successions aren't as long-range as you might like. What is your plan, *now,* if the current executive must leave soon for health or other reasons?

3. **Make sure your plan includes retirement funds for the executive.** Lack of retirement funds is a huge barrier to retirement—and underfunding is much more common than you might believe. Talk frankly with the management team about their retirement hopes, their retirement options, and their outlook financially.

   HANDS ON: Most large brokerage firms and many banks provide free retirement assessments. Talk to your banker or broker about coming to your organization and running one or more retirement planning seminars for key managers, no matter what their age. As many Boomers are finding out to their dismay, they should have started the process earlier.

4. **Create or expand your leadership development program.** You want a deep bench and, as Jim Collins found in *Built to Last,* the most successful organizations fill their top spots *from within.* So work on developing your best people. Not only will you have better management and leadership right away, but your best people will stay—because they will find that they can progress professionally.

HANDS ON: Hundreds of colleges and universities now have programs in nonprofit management. Find those nearest to you (see the Resources section at the end of this book) and talk to them about developing a program for your managers, perhaps at your organization's work site. No sense in reinventing the wheel. For example, the program at the Kellogg School of Management does this for a number of organizations.

5. **Make sure your board and key management team are fully aware of the executive's plans.** This item is specifically for executive directors. Do *not* sandbag your board on this issue. Talk to them openly and often (at least annually) about your plans, particularly if you are over fifty-five and planning either what is thought of as an "early retirement" (before sixty-two) or a career change. Remember to talk to your management team and lead as a steward.

FOR EXAMPLE: A very good friend of mine (who I'll call John) had led his organization for fifteen years and was considering his retirement options. At age sixty, John didn't want to leave: he loved the organization, his management team, and his job. He and I talked a number of times about his plans, and I urged him to both share his intentions with his board but, more important, to talk to his management team. John had developed the team to be frank and forthright with him so when he presented his plan (which was to stay on the job as long as he possibly could) he was surprised to see obvious frustration on the faces of a couple of his direct reports. He followed up with them individually and, after much discussion, realized that although they loved working at the organization, they were, essentially, waiting for him to leave so that they could get their shot at top leadership.

John called me and we talked about his dilemma for hours. He was deeply torn. He wanted to stay and knew that he did a good job. But he also knew if his key staff left he would be hurting his organization over the long run—something that he could not abide.

The organization's best interest won out, and John decided to leave in eighteen months, told his staff and board, and worked through a smooth transition. It was not emotionally easy on John or on the people he worked with, but it was, in John's opinion, the right thing to do for the organization and the people it served.

6. **When the executive goes, go—at least for a while.** I've watched probably five dozen transitions of long-serving executives to new ones, and the biggest (and very common) mistake the organization makes is to keep the exec on "in a consulting capacity" for some time. The idea is either to supplement the newly retired exec's income because her retirement was underfunded, or to ease her pain at leaving, or to provide support for the new exec, or all three. Resist. This is nearly always a mistake.

The staff need to learn how to deal with the *new* executive, without the easy access to the *former* one. The (now) former executive needs to go away, out of sight, out of mind, for a long period, one that I recommend be at least six months. If you want to pay your former executive, send her on a road trip to look at what peer organizations are doing around the country. Then have her come back and offer some ideas to the new executive and board in a written report and at a single meeting.

HANDS ON: Executives, when you retire, do your organization and your staff a favor. Go away.

Hopefully, your transition will be as smooth and painless as possible. But no matter what the age of your current executive, the changing demographics of your staff (more and more GenX and Gen@ and fewer and fewer Boomers) demand that you deal with the next big dilemma on staff: work-life balance.

Work-life balance

Boomers want it, but don't know how to get it, and are embarrassed to ask for it. GenX and Gen@, on the other hand, demand it, and do so without embarrassment. Hence, work-life balance is a key focal point of intergenerational conflict. Work-life balance is also a very important management issue, since the data show that we're working our staff to death—or at least to the door. Lastly, this is a financial concern: if staff want to work only fifty hours a week rather than sixty, and the work can't be automated or outsourced, who's going to do the work? And who is going to pay for it?

In looking at this issue, there are a number of things to keep in mind.

When it comes to work-life balance, everyone is right. That doesn't mean that only *you* and your perspective are right, it means *everyone* is right. Work-life balance, and related effects on a person and their family, is an *intensely personal* decision. There is no right or wrong answer. More than anything, you need to respect people's decisions to do with their life and their family what they feel is the best.

That's the key: *respect* their decision. Don't develop an attitude of scoffing at someone's decision to work more hours than you, or fewer hours, to attend their child's concert, or to miss it. This is their decision. You do what's right for you, and let them do what's right for them, without your comment.

I cannot emphasize this enough. I am sure you would never engage in, or tolerate, scoffing at someone's religious or spiritual beliefs, or their ethnic background, or their economic situation, or their race. This stuff is just as important and just as personal. Leave it alone.

Just because their work-life decision is right for them doesn't mean it's right for your organization. You'd be crazy to try to fully accommodate everyone's needs and wants, most of which will change over time. If you weren't crazy to try it, you'd be crazy about two years after you started. What's the first rule of nonprofits? Mission, mission, and more mission. The work *has* to get done. It may be able to be done more flexibly (see below) but it still has to get done. There is still the word "work" in work-life balance. So, for example, having flex hours may be great, but people need to attend staff meetings and be on site to help clients. A school may be flexible with faculty about their after-school duties, but teachers have to be in class when the students are. A nursing home may hire more part-time staff to accommodate people who want to work only part-time, but they still need people on site 24/7.

Thus, while demand from workers (of all generations) for a better and more flexible work-life balance is increasing, and while you definitely need to pay attention to it, the work still has to get done.

> **HANDS ON**: In recruitment, be open and specific about your expectations. If you have a place where everyone is expected to work sixty hours a week, including one full day on weekends, and where everyone is on call pretty much 24/7, say so. And say it up front. There is NO benefit in hiding this and having people come in and out through a revolving door.

Pay attention to trends and be as flexible as you can. GenX and Gen@ do want a better work-life balance than their parents. In pushing for that, they are causing their Boomer parents to rethink their own work-life balance. So, implement the Asking action, and find out what people want. Then, whether it is family leave, or flexible benefits, or more personal time, or working from home, think through what your organization can accommodate and do what you can.

> **HANDS ON**: Put together a work-life task force made up of staff of all ages, and a board member or two. Survey staff, and hold a focus group or two to find out what people are thinking about the work-life balance of the organization. Are you doing all you can? Are you saying what you actually do? As always, talk to peer organizations to see what they are doing in this area.

The Six Big Actions for Your Staff

Now that we've examined the four key impacts and discussed the pressing issues of executive transition and work-life balance, let's examine the Six Big Actions in relation to your staff. This is the first time we'll apply these actions (which were introduced in Chapter 3), and we'll return to them in all the chapters from here on.

Include generational issues in planning

For staff, generational issues need to be included in the following planning activities: financial planning (retirement benefits, flex benefits, restructuring staff to accommodate work-life balance issues, and so forth), succession planning, and mission capacity (ability to recruit and retain enough staff to do the mission). Make sure that generational sensitivity and forecasting go into your planning.

> **HANDS ON:** The best way to include generational issues in your planning is to include different generational representatives. Make sure you have representatives of all the generations on your planning groups and ask them specific questions about how your plans, goals, objectives, priorities, and strategies appear to them, not only professionally, but also as a representative of their age group. How would their peers react to this or that idea?

> **HANDS ON:** Younger staff often carry crushing school-loan debt. Thus, while capable, willing students may *want* to work with your nonprofit, they may not be able to afford to, unless you work with them on ways to reduce their debt, or defer it.

According to a 2006 study done by the Building Movement Project in New York, three out of four graduates entering the nonprofit workforce do so with significant educational debt, and the amount of such debt has risen 64 percent since 1993. Make sure you are both aware of this issue and the programs that exist to help graduates in this area. Your young workers will appreciate your awareness and sensitivity to a key issue of their generation.

Mentor and discuss among generations

Mentors are needed for new staff (of any age). And at various times, all staff need mentors for new technology, new challenges, or new methods of service provision. When mentors cross generations, mentoring can be a real barrier breaker and a real boon to your organization.

To develop mentoring programs, you'll need to have staff identify their key skills (their individual core competencies) and provide some training in good mentoring. *Note:* Staff shouldn't be forced to mentor other staff.

They can be asked, encouraged, or gently cajoled, but they really *do* need to volunteer.

Discussion groups are great ways to bridge barriers and develop cross-generational appreciation. Develop informal settings for discussion, such as brown bag lunches or field trips where you pair up with staff of different generations. If intergenerational conflict arises, you may need to bring in an outside facilitator to bring conflict to the surface and deal with it. But even in these situations, having a background of regular discussion will help.

Target market by generation

For staff, target marketing means asking about aspirations, work conditions, work-life balance, the value of your mission, and other aspects of their relationship to the organization. But it also means making sure that you can, in fact, give them what they want (to a certain degree) to retain them. It also means managing sometimes conflicting sets of wants. We already do this regularly—funders may well want different services provided, or in a different manner, than actual service recipients would prefer. We deal with such conflicts all the time.

You will almost always have generational staff differences about technology, benefits, work conditions, team building, socialization, work hours, and dress code. If the Boomers want everyone to wear, at a minimum, business casual, and the Gen@ staff see no reason not to come in every day in jeans, you have a conflict of wants.

The key is first to ask about these differences so that you can be aware of the various wants. Then use your increased discussion and intergenerational planning to bridge the divides that pop up. Common ground is almost always there if you can search for it together.

Age down

While aging down is generally a good thing, particularly with board and other volunteers, be very careful here. *Age discrimination is a crime,* and I am not suggesting that you ignore people for jobs just because they are Boomers, or members of the Silent Generation. In fact, we spend a fair amount of time in this chapter talking about how to successfully recruit, integrate, and retain Boomers coming in the door. So, this action is not about setting age goals, but rather about becoming more aware of the fact that aging down is going on naturally, and about being cognizant of the age mix. Just as the rural town with a rapidly increasing immigrant population needs to be aware of its ethnic diversity trends, you need to be paying attention to your generational mix at all levels of the organization.

You can actively age down the median age of volunteers by recruiting more younger candidates. Also age down your marketing, providing your message in ways that appeal to a younger audience. But the aging down of your staff is a natural process that will occur—if you let it.

> **HANDS ON**. The biggest danger here is the human tendency to hire what we're familiar with. This means if you are a Boomer, you will tend to hire more Boomers. If you are a GenXer, you'll tend to relate and hire more people of your generation. Ultimately who you want on your staff (and board, for that matter) is a group of people who reflect the adult age makeup of your community, (at least those between eighteen and seventy-five) and thus give you an entrée to, and perspective on, all age groups. Over time, if you try to be reflective of your community, your average staff age will come down slowly and steadily.

Meet techspectations

Meeting generational techspectations for staff requires that you have a mix of technology solutions available, because different groups have different needs. For example, you can have all of your forms, policies, staff surveys, meeting minutes, and the like available on your web site or intranet, *and* you can have them available in hard copy. This way, the Gen@ people feel at home, and the less techno-comfortable staff don't feel left out. You can advertise your positions online at places like Monster.com *and* put ads in the local paper. You can set up meetings with online scheduling *and* allow people the option of calling in their times.

While you can be generationally specific, you can't let tech laggards fall too far behind. The world is moving online, whether in accountability (most states want outcome measures and billings online) or oversight or things like electronic scheduling, presenting in PowerPoint, and so forth. Imagine if, ten years ago, you had let your Luddites not learn to type. Where would they be in a word-processed world? Thus, you need to gently pull even your tech resisters into the twenty-first century, but with sensitivity to resistance points.

The way to do this sensibly, with the lowest cost-to-outcome ratio, is to ask your staff (all of them) what they love and hate about your technology. Ask them how you think the organization can improve its use of technology. Ask them to pay attention to what technology is doing in other organizations and to bring ideas to you.

> **HANDS ON**: You can manage techspectations by asking Gen@ and GenX staff to mentor others. If your younger staff want to use more technology (perhaps a new piece of software that will ease work load), tell them fine, but they have to teach everyone how to use it. This presents a great opportunity for cross-generational bridge building or conflict, depending on how it is implemented and monitored, so think it through carefully and give the mentoring some oversight. Use your best mentors here.

Ask

If you've been in management for a decade or more, you may feel you know what your staff want. In truth, you probably do know three-quarters of what your staff wants. It's that last quarter you're missing. It's held back, it changes, and it varies from one generation to another. This last quarter holds the key to making your organization a great place to work, a great place to stay, and a great place to grow. You need to ask what staff want to discover to retain that recruitment and retention edge.

The act of asking is also the act of bridge building. If you care enough to ask, people realize it and appreciate it. It shows you care about them, their issues, and their perspectives. In the words of leadership guru John Maxwell, "Your staff don't care how much you know until they know you care."

Summary

In this chapter, we've covered the all-important issue of generational planning and intervention on staff. Employees are a key component of any nonprofit, and you need to accommodate, mentor, discuss, and focus on this issue if you are to move the organization successfully across the generational threshold, break down generational discord, and maintain effective mission momentum.

First, we went over the Four Impacts, and how they relate to staff. You learned that each of the Four Impacts has issues to deal with. Again, these are

- Boomers coming in the door
- Boomers going out the door
- Whatever happened to GenX and Gen@?
- Unintended consequences

Then we moved to the enormous issue of executive transition. To cope with this coming dilemma, I suggested you do the following six things to make the transition more successful.

- Assess the situation.
- Develop a contingency plan.
- Make sure your plan includes retirement funds for the executive.
- Create or expand your leadership development program.
- Make sure your board and key management team are fully aware of the executive's plans.
- When the executive goes, go—at least for a while.

The other looming generational issue is work-life balance. Here, I suggested the following:

- When it comes to work-life balance, everyone is right.
- Just because their work-life decision is right for them doesn't mean it's right for your organization.
- Pay attention to trends and be as flexible as you can.

Finally, we walked through the Six Big Actions, which are

- Include generational issues in planning
- Mentor and discuss among generations
- Target market by generation
- Age down
- Meet techspectations
- Ask

So, now you've looked at your employees and their generational issues in detail. I've often viewed the balance of nonprofit management as a tee-ter-totter, with staff on one end, board and volunteers on the other. Of course the executive director is the fulcrum, balancing the two groups on her head. Ouch.

We've dealt with staff. Your board and nongoverning volunteers are the subject of the next chapter.

| CHAPTER FOUR DISCUSSION QUESTIONS

1. What does our staff age breakout look like? How are our generations on staff changing?

2. Do we need to collect or update staff satisfaction information? Do we have adequate data on work-life balance?

3. How can we establish a mentoring program? Do we have enough staff turnover to merit this investment?

4. Do we see intergenerational conflict now? If it is present, how can we reduce it or prevent it in the future?

5. Are we doing enough asking in generational groups? What can we do better in this area?

5

Board and Volunteers

AS WE HAVE ALREADY SEEN, generational change will have many effects on our board and volunteers. These effects mean that your board and volunteers will begin to behave differently than you've come to expect. Similarly, their views of the organization will also not fit your expectations. This chapter will help you to understand the changes that will happen, prepare for them, and take advantage of them.

This chapter gets you started on the process of accommodating generational change in the areas of governing and nongoverning volunteers. This is the only chapter where we won't cover the Four Impacts directly, but rather as they relate to recruiting and retaining the best possible group of board members. (We'll come back to the Four Impacts in the remaining chapters.) There is a strong need for a new view of board volunteers, and the recruitment and retention of the best possible group of board members.

After looking at the board, we'll examine nongoverning volunteers. Some nonprofits get a large part of their work done through volunteers who are not on boards or committees (think Habitat for Humanity or Special Olympics). These volunteers have a somewhat different mind-set and a slightly different set of wants than governing volunteers, so we should have different, but still high, expectations of them.

Finally, we'll review the Six Big Actions in relation to board and volunteers.

A New Board Mind-set and Skill Set

I'm sure that at some point you've seen a kung-fu genre movie where the aged, wise master tells the young, enthusiastic student that "The key is your mind." In the original *Star Wars* movie Yoda told Luke to "feel the force." The point of these admonitions is that with big things, you've got to *believe* before you act. So, you must believe in the need, believe in the change, believe in your path.

On a more mundane level, all change management gurus tell us that the first step in initiating significant change is developing an organization-wide belief that *there is a need for the change.* This is the only thing that will overcome the normal inertia that most of us suffer from.

So, the first thing we have to do with the board is to make sure that their mind-set in all their deliberations includes generational change. Here are three specific things that boards can do in this area: embrace age diversity, reexamine their skill set, and begin succession planning for executive and board.

Embrace age diversity

Most nonprofits are always working on having an appropriately diverse board. You want to be ethnically diverse, you want to be representative of the different geographic communities you serve, you attempt to represent a variety of economic levels. Good for you; it's tough to do. Now it's time to add age (or generational) diversity to the mix. The first thing your board can do is establish a policy of reducing the average age of board members by actively seeking younger members.

> **HANDS ON**: In the Generational Self-Assessment (page 52), you calculated the average age of your current board. Save the number. Now, if you have the records, calculate the average age of the board five years ago. Then ten years ago. What's the trend? If your board is like most others, the average age has been increasing. Does the average age of your current board qualify for AARP membership (age 50)?

If so, you are almost certainly not representative of the age diversity of your community.

FOR EXAMPLE: I recently did a presentation on this issue to a board of a senior services organization in an area of the country that is a retirement mecca. One of the board members challenged me about my admonition about averaging down the age of the board to be more representative. "We are older people, we serve older people, our community is filled with older people. Why do we need younger people on the board? What can they bring us, and what can we give them? I don't get it."

A fair question, for sure. This organization does a large amount of work in the senior community, mostly with volunteers. One of the problems they were having was that their volunteer base was so old that the individual volunteers were not showing up for work because many were sick, some were dying, some were moving back to be near their children in other communities. I pointed out that the organization was seeking younger volunteers, and that the board was concerned about recruiting volunteers who are in their forties and thirties, but had no one on the board with that perspective. Additionally, I noted that it was important to the board members that the board have some legacy members, people who knew the history of the organization and its traditions. I asked them: "If your average age of board member is sixty-eight [which it was], who will be your legacy members in fifteen years? Better recruit them now, and recruit them young."

FOR EXAMPLE: A nonprofit in the Midwest had started out as a low-competition youth soccer league fifteen years earlier. Now it had grown into a youth sports league with both low- and high-competition divisions, and included soccer, basketball, softball, volleyball, and Ultimate Frisbee. The participants were from age five to fourteen. The organization had grown in size, complexity, and budget. But it had been difficult to recruit new board members and, as a result, most of the board members in 2005 were the same as the board members in 1990, the founding year.

The children of these board members were the first kids in the first soccer league and they were no longer age-eligible. When the organization began to have a falloff in applications for teams, they began to focus on marketing for the first time, with great difficulty. When I was asked to talk to the board and staff about marketing, the first question I had was "How many of your kids still play?" No hands went up. "How many of you have age-eligible kids?" Again, none.

"You need to get younger as a board," I said. "You need the perspective of a young parent, and you need to talk to the ten- to fourteen-year-olds who are at the age where they drop out of sports due to other commitments. You need to know the perspective of different age groups."

A certain amount of huffing and puffing ensued. People pointed out that *they* had been willing to drive kids to practices, *they* had been willing to be volunteer coaches, *they* had been willing to fundraise. They nearly literally threw up their hands in frustration. Likely they were a bit insulted that I insinuated that they were out of touch.

I assured them that younger parents still cared and that, by adding some younger board members, they could find out what the younger members' perspective was, what their peers were thinking, and what their kids were doing. I also told the present board that it wasn't that they were old—but fifteen years is a long time in terms of changing market wants.

Averaging down the age of your board will help ensure continuity, legacy, and perspective.

Reexamine the board's skill set

Given the changes that are occurring (and that we discussed in Chapter 3), you need to review the skills needed on your board (and perhaps board committees), followed by an analysis of where you are and where you want to be. This will help focus your recruitment efforts for new board members (which is discussed in more detail in the next section). It will also highlight the issue of generational change yet again with board and staff members.

HANDS ON: Here are some new things to consider as you develop your list of skills. These are not all-inclusive and will be developed at greater length in the section on board recruitment. Rather, these are the kinds of skills related to generational change that you may not yet have considered.

- **Generationally representative.** Do you have members from GenX, Boomers, Gen@, and the Greatest and Silent Generations all on your board?

- **Tech proficient.** Do you have at least two board members who are comfortable with new technology and its implications for your mission?

- **Media savvy.** Are your board members aware of what media people in their age group are reading, watching, and listening to? This is crucial for connecting with their generation.

- **Willing, capable mentors.** You need people (of all ages) who are willing to share and guide supportively—in other words, mentors, a key component of the Six Big Actions.

Note that all of the skills except the first are age-independent: you can fill any of these with people of any age. Adding these items to your skills list will make your organization more representative and better prepared for generational issues as they confront the board.

Succession planning for executive and board

We talked about this issue at length in the last chapter, but it is also a board issue, since the board hires, fires, and recruits the executive director. At some point, the board will have to deal with succession planning for the executive as well as board members. While this may not be fun and may even seem premature, it's necessary now. Even if your executive is thirty-five, you may face succession issues if he or she moves on to another job, or falls seriously ill or is suddenly disabled. Making this problem more acute for most organizations are two facts: Most boards don't have term limits; and most nonprofit staff have been forced to become very lean vertically, which means that there is often not a position (or person) being groomed to take over for the executive.

Here's how you can prepare.

Talk openly about succession planning. This is as important as buying insurance for your building or developing disaster plans if a tornado or flood hits your property. A number of good resources in the appendix address this issue directly, but remember that there are many barriers to good succession planning, some apparent, some hidden.

> **FOR EXAMPLE**: When I was on the board of a local human services organization in the mid 1980s our executive was also the founder. She had been on the job twenty-five years, was well past age seventy-five, and had been resisting any concept of retirement for years. She was a wonderful advocate for the developmentally disabled, probably the best advocate in state history, but at the same time the organization had grown from an annual budget of $500,000 to over $3,000,000 in three years, and we had long since passed her ability to manage the organization's new challenges.
>
> I was board vice president, soon to be president (we had a board succession process), and was told by the then president that I would be the guy to retire the executive. Why? Because the current president didn't want to confront her. Grreeeaaaat. Suddenly I was looking forward to being not president, but immediate past president, the job I would have after two years as president.
>
> As I looked more deeply into what had to happen, it became clear that not only did the executive not really want to go (although she was regularly talking about retiring) but that she had set things up financially so that we *couldn't* retire her. She had resisted ever letting the board put any money away for her retirement. How could we retire her with no pension? Obviously, we were over the proverbial barrel.
>
> My first week in office, I met with the executive and two other key board members and talked openly about retirement dates, what the current executive thought were needed attributes of her successor, whether there were any viable internal candidates (there weren't— another barrier), and what financial needs she predicted for herself

when she retired. I asked her to get back to us with her responses, and she said she'd think about it. I gave her a week, which may have seemed harsh but got the process rolling, and let everyone know we were going to deal with this on my watch. I wasn't going to pass this on to the next president.

I appointed three financial experts (two board members and an out-sider) to run down our financial options in quickly funding a pension for the executive. They came back with three options, of which the board chose one as its preference, and we set a retirement date for the executive of twelve months later—well into my second year as presi-dent, but six months before I went out of office.

The next eighteen months were difficult. Both the executive and cer-tain board members began to get ugly about the impending departure. At one board meeting, a motion was even made to fire the execu-tive—no pension, no financial security—on the grounds that she was undermining the process and the organization. I had to threaten to resign because I had made a personal promise to the executive that she would have a retirement fund if she went along with our plan and retired. The board backed off, but it was a close thing.

We survived, got a new executive who was fabulous, and moved on. The new leader made major changes, improved the organization, and left after three years. Transition executives are pretty common, and he did us a huge service. He passed the torch to a third executive who is also terrific. At this writing, she's been with the organization for over ten years.

HANDS-ON: Every year, at the time of the executive's evaluation, a small group of board members, including the board president, should talk with the executive about career and retirement plans. Having this regular discussion makes the subject less taboo, and there will be fewer, if any, ugly surprises. A board that I am on as this book is written has just such a discussion annually with our two key staff persons. It works wonderfully to ameliorate board concern that the staff members may suddenly leave, and lets the staff know we want them to stay. Surprise—open communications work!

Have board term limits, officer term limits, and a board succession plan. This provides for a regular turnover, new ideas, new perspectives, and more community networking, all of which are good. As far as succession, though, it also helps avoid the twenty-year term of a president, where the board says "What will we do without her?"

What does a plan like this look like? I recommend three-year terms for board members, with two sequential terms before leaving the board, sometimes permanently, sometimes just for a year or so. I recommend one-year terms for officers, with the understanding that most will serve in their office for two years. I also recommend having a vice-president who will, in nearly all cases, become president, and a vice-treasurer who will also nearly always become treasurer.

Taking a new approach to your board is, as we've seen, really establishing a new mind-set about the value, roles, and responsibilities of your board. Once you do that, it's much easier to be generationally sensitive and aware.

Recruiting and Retaining Excellent Board Members of All Generations

Now that we've looked at how to start thinking about generational issues in relation to our boards, we'll turn our attention to recruitment and retention. No matter what recruitment process you use, whether it is all done the week before the annual meeting or is an ongoing effort, you need to weave in generational issues. Here are some things to consider.

When you think diversity and skill set, add age and generational perspective into the mix. We talked about this earlier, but it bears repeating: no doubt your organization seeks ethnic diversity in its board, staff, volunteers, and donors. And you may already have a list of skills needed in your board skill set (for a few suggestions in this area, see page 86), but remember that the perspective of people of all ages is valuable.

Board recruitment is predictable, so plan. If you have term limits, and you know the skills you need as well as the skills you have (and when they will go off the board) this issue becomes reasonably predictable. Sit down with your board officers and nominating committee and talk through the issue. What do we need? What do we have? When will we need replacements? The table below illustrates board recruitment that attends to generational diversity as well as skills.

Sample Board Recruitment Grid

Skill/ representation	Board Member	Term Ends 2007	Term Ends 2008	Term Ends 2009	Priority Need
Legal	Jones	XX			XX
Fundraiser	Smith			XX	
Advocate	Adams		XX		
Banker	Burris			XX	
Businessperson	Keyes			XX	
County A					
County B	Jones	XX			XX
	Adams		XX		
Gen@	Smith			XX	
GenX					XX
Boomer	Jones	XX			
	Adams		XX		
	Burris	XX		XX	
	Keyes			XX	
Silent					XX

As you can see, the board has no GenX or Silent Generation members—only one Gen@, and four Boomers. This is typical. You can see the years that the board members' terms will end. The Priority Need column helps highlight the skills/representations that are either missing or that will be leaving the board soon. You can use a table like this to predict your needs, amend your board skill set, and recruit more successfully.

HANDS ON: There is a major problem with boards in the United States: the move from policy making to fundraising. More and more, boards are morphing from a group of people concerned with policy and supporting the organization to a collection of well-intentioned fundraisers. The cry of "Give, get, or get off!" overpowers all of the other important jobs that board members have. *If you are recruiting board members first and foremost for their ability to raise funds, you are making a big mistake.* Who will monitor management and hold it accountable? Who will be the liaison with the community (other than asking for money)? Who will help staff advocate for needed changes? Not the board—they are too busy worrying about charity golf outings and formal fundraising events.

Should board members be involved in fundraising? Absolutely. Should you have fundraising as a needed skill on the board? Of course. But when the primary function of the board is to "give or get," it's only a matter of time before the checks and balances that have served nonprofits so well for so long break down. Be careful.

If you are breaking a generational barrier, recruit more than one member at a time. This is particularly true for Gen@, but all people in all groups prefer the company of peers. Think about going into your first board meeting as a new board member. You are entering a private club. You may know one or two people, but if you are significantly younger than everyone else in the room, you will feel very out of place. So, give them a group if you possibly can.

Mentor, mentor, mentor. When you mix groups, by age, gender, ethnicity, or any other denominator, mentoring is crucial. Boards are no different. Mentoring helps build the board team, and helps you keep the board members you've recruited.

Here's what a board mentor program looks like in brief.

- Once a new board member is recruited, but well before their first meeting, the board president appoints or recruits a mentor. It is important to carefully select the mentor for the board member, but I don't favor automatically having the member be the same age, ethnicity, or background. That may happen, but does not *need* to happen to be successful.

- Before the first board meeting the new board member attends, the mentor sets up a dinner, coffee, or just a thirty-minute visit in the recruit's office. The agenda is simple: The mentor introduces himself or herself, goes over what will happen at the upcoming board meeting, reviews the board packet, explains how to read the financials, and answers any questions. The idea: have a friendly face at the meeting and reduce the mystery.

- At the first board meeting the recruit and the mentor enter together and the mentor takes the new member around to meet all the other board members. Then, for the next two, three, or even six meetings, the mentor sits next to the new member to provide easy access for questions.

- After the first two or three meetings, the mentor calls the new member to ask if there were problems, concerns, or questions.

- Some recruits will need more time, some less. Some will want that safety net of the mentor sitting next to them for six meetings, some will be fine after one. So, be flexible, but keep the intent—making the entry into the board culture less intimidating.

These tips will help you recruit and retain better board members of all ages, all backgrounds, and all perspectives. But what about nongoverning volunteers? That's next.

Recruiting and Retaining Multigenerational Volunteers

Now let's look at the other volunteers you use, the nongoverning volunteers. You already know that we turn out young volunteers in hordes by the end of college. You know that many Boomers are reaching retirement age and will be volunteering more. You also know the core concerns of each generation in terms of their wants, and that each generational group needs attention paid to the way they see the world. So let's spend some time looking at ways to recruit and retain volunteers from a generationally specific point of view.

One note on this area of your organization. Most likely, more and more nonprofits will need to fill more and more jobs with volunteers, sometimes highly trained ones. There simply is too much demand for services and not enough money to fill every need with paid staff. You may say, "Well, we do highly specialized work that no volunteer would do." Or even, "Our staff work on life-and-death issues. We need trained professionals for that."

Really? Did you know that most firefighters in the United States are volunteers? Certainly they deal with life-and-death issues. What about the physicians who staff Doctors Without Borders all over the world? They are certainly professionals, and highly skilled.

My point here is mainly to those of you who do not now widely use volunteers in your mission provision. Don't just skip this section or ignore this issue. My prediction is that in the next five to ten years, you will need to rethink your model of mission provision in a way that incorporates more—and more highly trained—volunteers.

Volunteer recruitment actions

Let's start with some things you can do to improve your volunteer recruitment and retention overall.

Ramp up your web site. No matter what age you are appealing to, most people are going to your web site first. Make sure that everything anyone would want to know about volunteering is online. Times, places, duration, responsibilities, and schedules should all be online, along with contact information by e-mail and phone. Provide links to online mapping software so that people can see the location of the work in relation to their own home or work site. You can even use RSS feeds (see more on this in Chapter 8) or e-mail alerts to inform potential volunteers of new opportunities as they arise. But get the information on the web, and *keep it current.*

Make your volunteering and volunteer management more professional. Back in 1991 in his seminal text on nonprofit management, *Managing the Nonprofit Organization,* Peter Drucker used the following phrase as the title to his chapter about volunteer management: "Going from Volunteer to Unpaid Staff." By this, Drucker indicated that we need to be more professional with our volunteers, and have more expectations of them. This means matching skills with needs and having written and oral expectations about showing up on time, appropriately dressed, ready to work, and able to work competently at the assigned job. It means job descriptions, lines of authority, and evaluations. It means reassigning volunteers to jobs for which they are more suited and, occasionally, firing them.

Is this a generational thing? No. It's a competence thing and a mission thing. And it will result, in the long run, in better volunteers doing better work for better mission. Hopefully, this is something you already do, and if you want to ramp up your volunteer management, there are resources for you in the Resources section.

Adapt your volunteer plans to suit Gen@. We're growing a very experienced generation of volunteers in high school and in college, but not getting them in the door as often once they are in the work world. Here are some things to think about in relation to recruiting Gen@ volunteers.

- *They are the most social animals ever*—so they want to volunteer with their friends. Develop volunteer experiences that can be performed in groups and facilitate that. Recruit volunteers from wherever people of this age congregate: from businesses, graduate schools, fitness centers, and the like. Work to accommodate groups.

- *Gen@s believe the opinions of their peers.* Want to go to a movie? Look at the reviews on RottenTomatoes.com. Thinking about buying a book? What are the reviews on Amazon.com saying? This age cohort values groups—and group opinions. So think through ways that you can post reviews of the volunteer experience from Gen@ online, or that you can hook up potential volunteers with experienced ones of the same age.

- *People in this age group want their time used efficiently.* This is particularly true for alumni of elite undergraduate and graduate schools. To get into such wonderful universities, these young people had to multitask most of their lives. They are, in the words of one midtwenties young man, "addicted to using our time efficiently." In this interview, he also spoke for a broad cross-section of his age peers: "Don't waste my time! I will happily come work for you for ten hours straight, and come back again, if it was fun and seemed worthwhile. But if you make me sit around for the first hour because you don't have your act together, I'll never come back, and neither will any of my friends." Here is where Gen@'s tendency to network and believe their peers (as noted above) can work to your favor—or detriment!

The Six Big Actions

Now let's look at the Six Big Actions in relation to our board and volunteer efforts.

Include generational issues in planning

I've shown you in this chapter how to plan for a better board, how to develop a new set of desired skills, and how to be generationally sensitive in your board and volunteer recruitment. Put this into action as quickly as you possibly can. The sooner you start to stretch the generational representation on your board and in your volunteer ranks, the better.

Mentor and discuss among generations

We discussed board mentoring in a fair amount of detail. But remember that nongoverning volunteers often need mentoring too. If your organization depends heavily on volunteers, take the time to develop volunteer mentors who can ease the way for new people. This will reduce turnover and increase volunteer satisfaction.

Target market by generation

Here as well, we've covered the key issues, but need to reiterate: *age discrimination is a crime.* Work to become generationally representative on your board, and perhaps recruit a bit harder for younger volunteers—but to turn someone away simply because they are too old or too young is unwise, unless there is a legal or administrative reason. For example, if you are providing meals for homebound seniors, your insurer would likely object to using teen drivers. You could use a seventeen-year-old to accompany an older driver to make the deliveries, but there could well be valid age-related reasons not to put the teen behind the wheel.

Age down

For nearly every organization, a general goal of getting a younger median age of board members and volunteers will help you. And, as you'll learn in the marketing chapter, this will almost certainly mean marketing in a fashion that appeals to younger people. Eventually, of course, this will happen on its own if you let it, just like with staff. One last admonition: If your board's average age is sixty, who is going to be on the board ten years from now to carry on your organization's traditions?

Meet techspectations

Board members' expectations about the use of technology often differ from those of your staff and clients. Ask the board about using online information, about printing out their own material before meetings (after you e-mail it to them), about all things tech, and then meet their expectations to the extent you can. Sometimes, you may get a tech backlash. Listen then too. One common complaint is about cell phones going off in board meetings.

> **HANDS ON**: An organization executive told me that she has printed on each board and committee agenda the following:
>
> I.   Call to Order
> II. Ceremonial Turning Off of All Cell Phones (with accompanying electronic music)
> III. Minutes of the last meeting
> IV. . . . .

The techspecations of most boards are rising, but be careful not to leave behind your nontechie board members (or those who may not have access to technology).

Ask

Asking is the least complex step in marketing, but for some reason, it is also the most difficult for some people to actually do. Board members and volunteers deserve to be asked and they deserve to be listened to. Find out why a board member is serving. Ask what he or she wants out of board service. Talk to volunteers about ways to make their volunteer service more fulfilling, and listen to their suggestions about making services to clients, patients, or students more effective.

It's easy for us "as the professionals" to disparage or ignore the input of our board. Bad idea.

> **FOR EXAMPLE**: A low-income housing nonprofit in the Southwest was growing rapidly. This nonprofit served many older people, and some of them were on the board. It had hired its first full-time techie, someone with excellent skills and incredible experience, especially for her age—twenty-eight. We'll call her Jane. Jane had finished her software degree by age nineteen, and had already been in the workforce most of a decade. She was not burdened with a lack of ego. She tended to brush off any suggestions on new software and new ways to use technology, particularly from the "old people" on the board. Jane attended and reported at board meetings, and regularly, in the Q & A part of her report, received suggestions on ways to improve the residents' use of and satisfaction with various tech improvements. Some of these ideas were good and some were pretty lame, but the ones that Jane needed to pay attention to were those from the board members who were also residents. Their perspective was invaluable.

Invaluable—except, apparently, to Jane, who basically ignored the suggestions, along with the ideas of one board member (we'll call him John). John always had suggestions, offering them quietly, and always in nontechnical language. Jane ignored the board and John until the day her boss finally had had enough. The boss called Jane into her office and asked why she was ignoring every idea the board put forth. This conversation ensued:

Jane: "Well, I'm sorry, but *look* at them. They're all old and really don't understand the challenges and nuances of tech. I really don't need their help. You hired me to do a job. Let me do it."

Exec: "Yes, you do need their help, and I will NOT tolerate your condescension to these people. They are first and foremost your ultimate bosses. Second, they are volunteers, who willingly give of their time for our mission. Third, their perspective counts. We need to know what people outside our offices think, whether its about services or technology. Lastly, some of them DO have great technical skill, but you are so focused on their age that you won't even give them a chance."

Jane: "And who would these tech wizards be? I certainly haven't noticed anyone speaking geek."

Exec: "Well, start with John."

Jane: "John? I admit he's always making suggestions, but he does it in nontech language. Not very impressive."

Exec: "Just so you know, he's chair of the computer sciences department at the university. He speaks in plain language so that the rest of us can understand him. You might want to listen a bit more closely, and consult with him now and then."

Your board and volunteers are a market. They deserve to be listened to.

Summary

In this chapter, we've looked at a variety of issues and concerns surrounding generational change and your board and nongoverning volunteers.

First, we looked at the need to embrace a new mind-set toward boards and volunteers. This includes taking the following actions:

- Embrace age diversity
- Reexamine the board's skill set
- Succession planning for the executive and board

Next, we turned to recruiting and retaining excellent board members. This task, which is no small effort, includes the following suggestions:

- When you think diversity and skill set, add age and generational perspective into the mix
- Board recruitment is predictable, so plan
- If you are breaking a generational barrier, recruit more than one member at a time
- Mentor, mentor, mentor

Then, we looked at the recruitment and retention issue through the increasingly important lens of volunteering. Here, I noted that you need to put everything about volunteering online, and professionalize your volunteering management—hold people to higher expectations and prepare for more volunteers as demand increases and funding stagnates. We also looked at specific ways to recruit across generations.

Finally, we went through our Six Big Actions in relation to boards and volunteers. Many of these had been covered in part earlier in the chapter, but one thing I pointed out was to listen to your board, and not fall into the trap of thinking "I'm the professional," and thus too smart to listen to the nonprofessional.

Remember that your board and volunteers are key elements in any generational planning and strategy. You need these people to be as generationally representative as your staff, perhaps even more so. Why? Because they are your link to the community, to the people you serve. This is the subject of our next chapter.

CHAPTER FIVE DISCUSSION QUESTIONS

1. Do we have a good age diversity and representation on our board and in our volunteers? How can we do better?

2. How can we keep the pipeline of younger volunteers full? Who do we need to be in touch with—high schools, colleges, military organizations, church youth groups?

3. What can be done to accommodate our older board members and volunteers as well as our younger ones? How can we give both a sense of community?

4. What about mentoring on the board? How can we use that with our other volunteers, and perhaps with our new staff?

6

The People You Serve

WHAT'S THE FIRST RULE OF NONPROFITS? Mission, mission, and more mission. To this point, we've been talking about mission enablers and mission providers: staff, board, and volunteers. But now we turn to the reason you exist: the people you serve. The Boomers, GenXers, and Gen@s are just as prevalent in your service community as they are on your staff—or are they? That's an issue we'll deal with. And, unlike our discussion of staff and board, which mostly dealt with the three generations I just mentioned, service recipients are more likely to also be Silent Generation or Greatest Generation members, so we'll discuss those generations in more depth here as well.

In this chapter you will see how the Four Impacts affect your service recipients, as well as how the Six Big Actions can help you adapt for the people you serve.

We'll address ways to determine what your future service recipients will look like, and we'll assess how generational change will affect this area. And, we'll also look at possible service accommodations and what some agencies are doing to make sure they are sensitive to generational change—and how they're even ahead of this crucial curve.

By the end of this chapter you should have a pretty good handle on the service side of the generation equation, and be ready to ramp up some other specific skills and resources.

The Four Impacts and the People You Serve

Once again, we start with the Four Impacts: Boomers in the door, Boomers out the door, GenX and Gen@, and unintended consequences. These affect everything—that is no less true for services than it is for staff, marketing, or finance. Let's take a look.

Boomers coming in the door

If by this point you are wondering why everything seems to revolve around the Baby Boomers, get over it. In demographic terms, it does. In financial terms, it does. In marketing terms, it does. And in service terms, it does.

But wait, you say . . . our organization does not target Boomers. We're all about twenty-somethings, or about children, or about teens. We don't serve Boomers. This doesn't matter for us.

Actually, it does. The Boomers are so big (as a group), so darn self-absorbed, so focused on getting their way (which they pretty much always have), that, as I said in the second chapter, they are going to suck up more and more resources. And here is where Boomers coming in the door matter (even if it's not *your* door).

If you do serve Boomers, or if your plan is to serve them, get ready for a lot of clients who are very, very demanding. If you don't serve Boomers, better get ready to serve the generations you do focus on *with fewer resources*—because the people who help the Boomers are going to get the majority of the pie.

Either way, in your strategic, marketing, and financial planning, Boomers will have a huge impact.

Boomers going out the door

Of course, if your target market is Boomers, and they are leaving, you've got some bumps ahead. What kind of nonprofit might this affect? Health clinics, symphony orchestras, museums, nonprofit social clubs and fitness centers—any place that takes time to build up a loyal group of voluntary customers (people who have the choice to not come in or go elsewhere) are at risk when Boomers leave. Boomers are retiring and moving to other communities, and it takes a long time to replace them. (Of course, nonprofits who serve Boomers who are retiring to retirement centers have the reverse problem.)

For any nonprofit, volume of service, that is, the number of clients (patients, students, parishioners) is a key metric. How will the transition of the Boomers from workers to retirees affect you? Do you need more capacity? Less? A different mix? And, while we're at it, how will it affect your donations? Will Boomer retirement mean people are moving away, or moving to your community? Or will they stay put but change life patterns?

> **FOR EXAMPLE**: When people retire, most change their daily routines, particularly giving up the commute to and from work. They don't hang out at the same places for lunch, they don't fill up their cars at the same gas stations, they patronize different quick marts, and so on. It may also mean they change the patterns of the nonprofits they patronize. If, for example, you live in the exurbs but work downtown, you may well use the downtown YMCA for your lunchtime workout. Once you retire, will you still come all the way downtown to go the same Y?

Here's another question: Will retirement income (usually less than full-time employment) result in fewer donations or a decrease in the size of donations? Donations are closely tied to service provision. No one knows what retirement will mean for donations. You may remember a few years back there was much hubbub about the huge transfer of wealth that would occur as Greatest and Silent Generation members died out and their estates passed to their Boomer children. The prediction was that this would result in huge influxes of cash, stocks, and real estate to (mostly) larger nonprofits, such as hospitals and universities. I first saw this prediction in 1998. In 2006, data in the *Chronicle of Philanthropy* shows there had been no noticeable increase from the predicted transfer. So much for all the hubbub.

There is no widespread agreement on the effect a generational retirement in the Boomers will have on their charitable giving. For one thing, their retirement will take place over about twenty years, so it's not going to happen overnight. But Boomers regularly surprise the experts with their behavior. So, watch carefully, and look at your donation funds. Are they being provided by Boomers? If so, pay even more careful attention.

Whatever happened to GenX and Gen@?

If your services are focused on GenX or Gen@ individuals, are you seeing a lower number than when you were Boomer-focused? Why? After all, though the Boomers totaled about 80 million Americans at the last census, Gen@ is not far behind with 75 million. So where are they?

The answer is that they're in groups. Recall that these two generations, particularly members of Gen@, love groups, trust groups, value the advice of their peers, and are used to getting advice instantly, through instant messaging online or texting on their cell phones. So, if you are having difficulties attracting or retaining GenXers or Gen@s, it may be because you aren't reaching them in the way that's most effective for their cohort.

Reaching Gen@ and GenX is a matter of word of mouth. It may well be a tough sell to get the first Gen@ member in the door, but if they are happy with your organization, the next twenty Gen@ members will pour through the door in a heartbeat. The younger the age you are trying to serve, the more you need to work through peers to attract them.

And here's the hint . . . that peer doesn't have to be a friend (though it helps). It can just be another person their age. This is why online reviews, blogs, and discussion groups are so popular and so vital to decision making in the younger generations. And that includes the decision to use your services.

> **FOR EXAMPLE**: In preparing to write this book, I conducted a number of focus groups by generations. My Gen@ group, made up primarily of early to mid twenty-somethings, was asked, among other things, to react to this scenario:
>
> *"You read about a place to see art, or to get a health checkup, or to go to audit a class. What do you do now? Do you go check it out, or . . ."*

Below are the responses. The italics are my words, and more than one quote means more than one person was answering. Some answers are compressed or combined for the sake of flow.

"I'd go online and check it out." "Yep." "Absolutely."

"How?"

"Go to the web site, Google the organization, you know, check it out."

"What would you be looking for? Can't be just a cool logo!"

"I'd be looking for other people's comments. If the site has a review section, or a blog, or a discussion group, and see what real people thought. I'm kind of immune to promotion on a web site."

"Yeah, the place may look cool, but what do people who've been there really think?"

"There are so many places to go. I'm not going to waste my time going someplace that hasn't been checked out first."

"But someone has to be first. . . ."

"Not me." "No way." "Absolutely not."

"When you say 'real people,' who do you mean?"

"People my age, y'know, not old people. I mean, old people are cool and all, but I care about what people my age think a lot more."

"OK, but what if the web site doesn't have reviews, or blogs, or that kind of commentary on it? What then?"

"Well, I might ask my friends by phone or IM, but I would certainly Google up other places like the one I was checking out and compare . . ." "Yeah, me, too. No point in just looking at one place."

"I might go look up a discussion group on the subject, like art, or health care, and post a question about the organization as well. I usually get pretty quick feedback from that kind of thing, too . . ."

"And, if you decided to give the place a try, what then?"

"Get a bunch of people and go check it out . . ."

So, there you are. With the ability to get instant comparisons, feedback from peers, and look at all their options quickly, getting Gen@ members (and to a lesser extent GenXers) in the door is difficult. But when you get one person, you get a lot of people.

Unintended consequences

There are dozens of ways you can have unintended consequences in services, whether it's in treatments that hurt rather than help (think thalidomide in the 1960s), or providing a service that solves the problem so completely that you no longer have a service base (think polio in the 1950s).

In the generational context, though, the biggest and, frankly, most likely unintended consequences are of being unaware of what different generations want, and assuming that all customers are the same.

Ask yourself this: does a college freshman at eighteen want the same thing as a college freshman at twenty-four who has just finished her hitch in the Navy? While both seek an education, the latter has worked a tough job for six years and is most likely more focused, disciplined, and has a better knowledge of herself. Similarly, does an alcoholic at age twenty-five want the same thing as an alcoholic at age forty-five? Both want to learn how to manage their addiction, but the way they are treated and their motivations to stay in recovery will be very different due in part to their ages.

Unfortunately, most nonprofits are making a significant push to *standardize* their mission output (their services) so that it is more measurable, more "scalable" (they can provide services more efficiently, like a factory), and costs less to provide on a unit basis. The unintended consequence of standardization is that you may well please no one generation fully—and you can't afford to lose a single person you serve in our increasingly competitive world.

We'll look more at this issue and its solution in the chapter on marketing.

What Will Your Service Recipients Look Like?

The people you provide service to—and the cultural context they live in—are changing rapidly. In this section, we'll first look at how they are changing generationally, and then at two major cultural shifts (first noted in Chapter 2) that you'll have to account for: increasing diversity and redefining the family.

As you grapple with the many effects of generation change, you need to consider how your service recipients break out generationally—both now and, more importantly, in five to fifteen years. The first step is to figure out where your organization is now generationally, and then look at some projections for the future. You need to do that for your community in general and then for your organization's specific service recipients. A number of resources listed in the Resources section can help you examine your larger community, but I recommend these places to start: U.S. Census; state, county, or city government; and trade associations and mission advocacy organizations.

- **U.S. Census**: www.census.gov/. Start with the American Community Survey (under the People & Households category), and drill down. You can find information by age, country of origin, income, marital status, even characteristics of people who speak a language other than English in the home. All great information and updated every year (in projection form) in addition to the decennial census.

  FOR EXAMPLE: Following is a table from the Census web site. It shows data estimates for 2003 for age groups by gender in Illinois. I got this information in seven clicks, and could have sorted by county, by congressional district, and other ways. The generations for these groups have been added to the left of the table. Note that the Census does *not* group people by generations, so you'll need to do that yourself. If you want to look for trends in population, you can also compare these groupings with data from previous census years.

Sample Population by Age Group

Population by Gender and Age Group in Illinois as of 2003

		Estimate	Lower Bound	Upper Bound
	Total:	12,328,721		
	Male:	6,033,866		
	Under 5 years	450,472	445,823	455,121
	5 to 9 years	463,555	449,314	477,796
	10 to 14 years	468,971	455,228	482,714
Gen@	15 to 17 years	264,858	260,638	269,078
	18 and 19 years	151,957	147,823	156,091
	20 years	85,151	77,824	92,478
	21 years	77,215	69,473	84,957
	22 to 24 years	256,772	246,134	267,410
	25 to 29 years	425,505	419,555	431,455
GenX	30 to 34 years	457,326	451,842	462,810
	35 to 39 years	444,748	429,913	459,583
	40 to 44 years	493,531	479,349	507,713
Boomer	45 to 49 years	459,863	453,008	466,718
	50 to 54 years	395,577	391,861	399,293
	55 to 59 years	319,896	310,203	329,589
	60 and 61 years	102,344	94,076	110,612
	62 to 64 years	131,029	122,858	139,200
Silent	65 and 66 years	77,344	70,612	84,076
	67 to 69 years	98,876	93,632	104,120
	70 to 74 years	153,218	146,136	160,300
	75 to 79 years	123,127	114,091	132,163
Greatest	80 to 84 years	77,724	72,090	83,358
	85 years and over	54,807	47,827	61,787
	Female:	6,294,855		
	Under 5 years	436,235	430,979	441,491
	5 to 9 years	437,942	424,254	451,630
	10 to 14 years	440,297	426,174	454,420
Gen@	15 to 17 years	255,285	251,491	259,079
	18 and 19 years	142,266	138,234	146,298
	20 years	73,990	66,780	81,200
	21 years	72,390	64,091	80,689
	22 to 24 years	258,799	249,213	268,385
	25 to 29 years	427,276	422,153	432,399
GenX	30 to 34 years	462,600	457,320	467,880
	35 to 39 years	460,079	443,324	476,834
	40 to 44 years	500,912	484,915	516,909
Boomer	45 to 49 years	474,270	469,952	478,588
	50 to 54 years	415,655	411,361	419,949
	55 to 59 years	333,978	321,895	346,061
	60 and 61 years	123,105	114,734	131,476
	62 to 64 years	153,377	144,914	161,840
Silent	65 and 66 years	97,381	89,180	105,582
	67 to 69 years	128,411	121,017	135,805
	70 to 74 years	180,823	172,566	189,080
	75 to 79 years	176,046	167,316	184,776
Greatest	80 to 84 years	128,772	122,217	135,327
	85 years and over	114,966	106,495	123,437

- **Your state, county, or city government.** These are the people who are responsible for your locale, and they *should* have more focused information sets. Some states have a state demographer who can help you track information. Some local agencies just draw their data from the U.S. Census, where the work will already be done. Go to the governmental unit's web site, or call or e-mail them. *Note:* If your organization serves a particular part of the community that is "assigned" to a state agency, such as health care, aging, welfare recipients, and so forth, also try those agencies for good data and data projections.

- **Your trade or mission advocacy association.** At either the state or national level, the trade association or mission advocacy association that your organization belongs to will, in all probability, have some data to make its case to your state legislature or the U.S. Congress, or both. For example, if you are a retirement center, you have trade associations for that industry, but if you are thinking about providing more services for Alzheimer's patients, you could check with the Alzheimer's Association. Both the trade and advocacy groups will be excellent sources of data.

Try to get information that allows you to project your community trends by generation. You may just want to have one or two groupings, but if you use my generational definitions, remember these birth years:

Greatest Generation: Born 1901–1924

Silent Generation: Born 1925–1945

Baby Boomers: Born 1946–1962

GenX: Born 1963–1980

Gen@: Born 1981–2002

If yours is a communitywide organization that provides public education, advocacy, or other services to benefit the community at large, this level of detail is probably where you'll stop. For example, environmental groups, or those that advocate for better housing or public education, would not need data beyond this. But if your organization is like the majority of 501(c)(3) organizations, it works at the individual level. Therefore, you need to look directly at *your* service recipients. First, gather what data you have by age.

Are you keeping intake or attendance or donation records with age data? If so, just review that data and group people by generation. Dull but important work.

If you are not gathering data with either age or year of birth, you need to make some estimates for the present, and then start collecting better data. You can get surprisingly good estimates from your employees if you get them together, ask them specific questions, and average their responses (assuming there are more than five employees).

HANDS ON: Assemble your staff and discuss the need to accommodate the people you serve given their generations. Come prepared with a brief survey to hand out to the staff. That survey should look something like this.

Note: This example assumes a survey date of 2008, with the ages in each generation stated accordingly. If you are doing this earlier or later than 2008, make the necessary adjustments.

Generational Estimate: 7/15/2008

We are trying to get an estimate of the people we serve by generation, to be increasingly sensitive to generation-specific wants and needs. We don't currently collect this information but will be starting soon. For now, we need your help to estimate where we are, as a benchmark for the future. We understand that you will be estimating age, which is difficult, but if we all make the estimate, the average will be accurate enough to use.

Please estimate the percentage of the people we serve who are in the following age groups:

          Over 84: _____%

          63–83: _____%

          46–62: _____%

          28–45: _____%

27 and under: _____%

(The total should be 100%)

(Remember, you may have to do a quick lesson in percentages for any staff who have forgotten their high school math!)

The next step is to develop ways to collect age (or better yet, birth year) information on different service populations. This will allow you to look at trends, hopefully anticipating major shifts in population ages.

Here is a sample display for a midsized church. They collected information over a six-year period. The church has three Sunday morning services. They offer a more traditional service as the first service, followed by two contemporary services. The church has just recently started offering small group discussions. They have had two sequences, labeled below as Group I and Group II. For comparison, the bottom row of the table shows each generation's percentage of the total church membership.

Percentage of Attendance by Generation

	Greatest	Silent	Boomers	GenX	Gen@
Worship:					
First Service (Traditional)	22%	31%	28%	15%	4%
Second Service (Contemporary)	3%	6%	54%	29%	8%
Third Service (Contemporary)	1%	8%	47%	29%	15%
Small Groups:					
Group I	2%	8%	35%	50%	5%
Group II	2%	10%	34%	45%	9%
Sunday School	10%	16%	47%	22%	5%
Generation as Percent of Total Membership	7%	14%	46%	21%	12%

Note that the younger people flock to the latter, contemporary service, but not the first, more traditional one. The reverse is true for the older parishioners. The Boomers dominate everything, except the small groups, which seem to be a place that the GenX members congregate. It appears that the older population doesn't care much for the small groups.

With this data in hand, the church can explore a number of questions about how well it serves each generation and what kinds of activities to provide. For example, should the church offer more discussion groups? Should it focus on attracting older members to join small groups? Should it focus on the small groups as a means of making sure that the GenX members continue to get what they are seeking from church?

This kind of information is invaluable as you look at what works, what doesn't, what's changing, and what needs attention.

This approach will get you started. Then you will need to begin to find a way to collect information by age, if not for every single person you serve, then for a representative sample. Once you do this baseline assessment, you will be ready to consider where you are and how you may need to adjust and reconfigure your services to accommodate the new information.

Increased diversity and redefining family

While the changing generations are going to influence what your service recipients will look like in the near future, two other widespread cultural phenomena will also have an effect. We discussed these in Chapter 2, but they need special review here since they affect planning. These trends are *increased diversity* and *redefining family*.

Increased diversity. The population in the United States, and to a similar extent in Europe, is becoming more diverse by the day. This diversity, along with strong ethnic pride, presents tremendous challenges for nonprofits that are underfunded and overworked. But understanding the cultures in your community is key to being able to market to them, provide services they appreciate, and successfully pursue your mission.

> **FOR EXAMPLE:** I recently walked into our local Walgreens to pick up a prescription and heard a recording that said: "Welcome to Walgreens. If you have questions, our pharmacists can help you in these languages: Vietnamese, Thai, Spanish, Russian, Chinese, Korean." I was really impressed. Given Walgreens' national reach and deep pockets, you can probably trust that those languages are the most common

and fastest growing in the United States. While it may be a different mix in your community, these are a really good place to start.

Walgreens is a great company, constantly innovating and staying on top of what's wanted in their communities. That's why it is on the list of great companies studied by Jim Collins in his best seller *Good To Great*. Imagine what Walgreens can do if it can capture the "immigrant, not-yet-speaking English" market.

But remember that language proficiency is not cultural competence. Cultural competence goes much deeper, mandating a much greater investment of time and effort on the part of the management and staff. Rural, suburban, or urban, all communities are becoming more diverse, a fact that crosses generations.

Now imagine what your organization can do relative to the cultures it now serves and those you can expect to arrive in the next five to fifteen years.

Redefining family. This second trend also crosses generations, and also affects the ways services are delivered. I was recently part of a discussion with nonprofit human resources directors who agreed that they have more and more employees in their thirties who are grandparents, and taking care of their grandchildren because the mothers are still in high school. "Grandparents. In their thirties?" I asked. "My wife and I didn't have our first child until the month before I turned thirty!" The HR experts agreed—first, that I was clueless, and second, that in their field they see more and more of a young-grandparent trend, as well as other changes that have direct consequences on HR policies: the growth of single-parent homes, blended families, stay-at-home dads, a "daddy track" as well as "mommy track," multiple entries and exits from the workforce related to family care needs, and so forth. While the example above is, on the surface, about employees of some nonprofits, guess what? Some of them are probably also *served* by a nonprofit in their community too. What's clear is that the traditional two-parent, one-marriage family, while still the majority, is no longer the "norm." This reconfiguration has clear generational impact. People have to change career and retirement plans to help take care of family needs.

Just as HR policies need to change to reflect these changes, service provision needs to change. So, carefully consider how the reconfigured family affects the people you serve.

Reconfiguring Your Services

The decision to reconfigure services happens at the intersection of mission (as expressed in service delivery) and marketing. In Chapter 7, we'll examine the marketing cycle, where you'll see that once you identify your markets and find out what they want, only then do you create, amend, or reconfigure your services. So, read this section with the understanding that the final decisions about service design need to be made with the marketing input you'll gain when you follow the steps in Chapter 7.

When you identify a generational divide (a significant difference between, say, Boomers and Silent Generation) in your service population, the next step is to look at what the different generations want and consider the following issues:

- Does our mission need to be revisited to incorporate this generational issue?

- Are either or both of the generations across this divide a target market?

- Is the generation a target market in itself (i.e., Boomers, Gen@s, and so forth)?

- What does the generation I'm serving want?

- What is the cost of accommodating this generational issue?

- What is the long-term (five- to ten-year) benefit to our organization and our mission if we change to accommodate the generational issue?

Only after these questions have been asked and answered can you really decide what to reconfigure, change, add, delete, modify, or accommodate.

Finding out what people want requires asking. When you ask, you'll learn a lot that you can accommodate to, and that is the essence of marketing—

giving people what they want. But this challenges nonprofits. I regularly hear executives respond to this advice with, "I don't want to get on a treadmill of change, change, change. Our people can't handle it." The fact is, *we have to change constantly* to keep up with the wants of our markets, but that change does not have to be huge or seismic in nature.

Change in response to generational wants doesn't have to mean earthquakes in service. It's often better to improve service 1 percent a day, every day, than to shoot for big change. When you do that, you get in the habit of making improvements, but no single change is big enough to kick in the "resistance to change" demon that vexes so many of us.

> **FOR EXAMPLE**: An animal shelter in a small town that has become a retirement mecca has recently adapted to fit the town's generational change. The small community's population is rapidly aging (in terms of its median age) and the staff are seeing more and more retired folks coming in looking for pets to adopt. After some customer complaints, the executive realized that his staff—who were mostly Gen@s—were not communicating well with the senior customers. He talked to his staff, and everyone went through training to learn how to talk more slowly, speak up, look the customer directly in the face, and not show any signs of irritation if they took a bit longer than other customers to complete their business.
>
> The result? Word came back pretty quickly that the organization "had the nicest young people on their staff," and the shelter staff were invited to come to speak at senior functions. Bottom line—pet adoptions went up. Mission accomplished—literally.
>
> **FOR EXAMPLE**: A museum in Florida, near a large university, had purchased a large quantity of "portable tour guides," the headsets that teach you more about an exhibit at your own speed. A great innovation. But the museum had a "split market." They had two major market segments: college and grad students, particularly art students, and senior citizens. Complaints about the new headsets came from two directions. Seniors said they couldn't hear the words on their headsets,

while students said the recordings were boring and that the headsets "looked old."

The museum responded with a number of small changes that added up to much higher customer satisfaction (which they measured). First, with the ubiquity of iPods and other MP3 players, they offered the "tour" as a set of podcasts that could be downloaded right at the museum, or from the museum web site. Thus, the younger customers could use their own equipment. Second, they made sure that any standard headset would fit their portable audio device. Again, the younger people could use their own equipment, or choose from a broader selection. This choice allowed the senior customers to select headsets that were more comfortable, reduced background noise, and didn't conflict with the fairly common issue of hearing aids. Finally, the sets were reconfigured to allow for a higher volume option.

One key part of this story is that the museum didn't figure out on their own that a problem existed: they asked, asked regularly, and listened to their customers. I'm sure you often hear about "adding value" to a service, but it's only added value if the customer thinks so. Let's suppose that the museum added music to the background of their tour recordings, assuming that people like music. They would be right and wrong. People do like music, *but they like the music they like,* and if you have teenagers or college-age kids, you know how important this is to most of them. In addition, the seniors already were complaining about not being able to hear . . . so it's pretty likely that adding music would reduce the value of the service for them. Always ask.

MeBranding

As noted in Chapter 2, "MeBranding" is the desire to have services and products provided in the exact, unique way that an individual wants them. This can have a major influence when reconfiguring services. Despite limited resources, nonprofits do need to think about making services *more* flexible and giving service recipients more choices. The choices offered should be a result of asking the generation you are accommodating to.

MeBranding is present in every generation, but the expectation of it is greater the younger your service recipients are. Thus, you can go a long way toward getting a more satisfied Gen@ customer if you offer a few choices—while fewer (or no) options may be needed to please a Greatest Generation customer. Remember, Greatest Generation members were focused on service in large homogenous groups, respecting authority, and doing what they were told. In general, they don't need or want too many options. In contrast, Gen@s grew up with nothing but choices in front of them, and they are both very good at making choices and they *expect* some customization (watch them whip through a ten-page restaurant menu, or choose thirty songs from their music library of ten thousand songs to make up a playlist). If you are set on a one-size-fits-all service array, expect less happiness in the Gen@ people you serve than in the Greatest Generation service recipients.

One more thing about MeBranding: the wants of the markets change faster than you can survey, particularly when you get to Gen@. That does not mean you shouldn't survey or ask, but it does mean you need a second line of accommodation: your staff.

> **HANDS ON**: Train, talk to, mentor, and role model flexibility with your staff in relation to the people you serve. This is a key element of customer service in multigenerational environments and, again, particularly if you serve a younger population. Tell your staff, "If someone asks you for a reasonable accommodation, be reasonable in your response. Don't start with 'No!' or 'We don't do that.' Think before you answer: *Is there some way we can accommodate this request, even just in part?* Be creative in your solutions."

Then, as the supervisor, you need to praise and support accommodations that pop up, even if they aren't the best solution. Even in the worst case, where someone accommodates in a far too expensive or disruptive way, praise the fact that they tried to accommodate, and work on helping them pick better ways next time.

Also, as you train your staff, ask them to turn the situation around and look at their own expectations. When they ask for an accommodation—when they make a MeBrand request ("I'd like the dressing on the side." "Could I get the 'special' with no mayo?")—what expectation do they have? Of a polite answer? Of course. Of an attempt to meet their wants? Absolutely. The same holds true for the people your staff serve.

Training in this area is key: The Ritz-Carlton chain of hotels has, at this writing, a policy of authorizing any staff person to spend up to $2,000 on the spot to fix any guest problem or concern. Since the Ritz has had this policy for twenty years and is not in bankruptcy, you can see that their intense training of staff in how to make accommodation choices (and spend the money) has paid off.

MeBranding is choice run amok, but it is a very real part of the society we live in. As I wrote this section, I thought about all the combinations of choices I see when I travel:

Hotels: smoking or nonsmoking room, one bed or two, ground floor, high floor, late check-in or not, crib, sleeper sofa, single or suite, accessible room.

Airlines: first class, business, economy, window or aisle, special meal (which more and more means your choice of plain or salted(!) pretzels), search flights based on schedule or price, direct, one-stop, multistop.

Rental cars: compact, economy, midsize, full size, SUV, van, GPS, satellite radio, car seat, insurance or no, purchase the gas or not.

So, lots of choices. Almost like going to a specialty coffee shop. Then I thought about a few nonprofits in our town. Let's look at the choices they offer.

Symphony orchestra: Ten years ago, all you could get was full symphony concerts or pops concerts, either in single concert purchases or season tickets for one or the other, but no mixing. Now, you get pops, chamber orchestra, full symphony, community outdoor concerts, and you can mix and match your purchases any way you want. More choices, more mixing, more customization. And you can order tickets online. Grade: B+.

Human service agency: Wide array of services, but once you walk in the door, you get the services they deliver the way they deliver them. I've been around this organization for twenty years as a volunteer and very, very little has changed. Other than scheduling choices (always 10 a.m.–4 p.m., Monday–Thursday), you have very, very little choice, even in the counselor you see. Oh, and you can't make an appointment online. Grade: D.

The comparison is not quite fair, of course. The travel industry has deep pockets and a great incentive to compete by accommodating various wants. The symphony has much, much more flexibility (with its funds coming from donations and ticket sales) than does the human service agency (with funds, oversight, licensing, and regulation coming from the government and/or insurers). Even so, the culture of the human service organization is "my way or the highway," and when I look at the age of its customer base, it's primarily over sixty, or from people who have no financial choices. What will they do in ten years when their market is over seventy?

What will *you* do? What *can* you do? Lots, as you'll see when we explore the Six Big Actions in relation to the people you serve.

The Six Big Actions and the People You Serve

While we've seen the benefit of the Six Big Actions in working with your staff, board, and volunteers, you may wonder what application they will have to the people you serve. Let's examine one by one the help these actions can give you.

Include generational issues in planning

At the beginning of most planning efforts, there is some kind of situational analysis, usually called a SWOT (Strengths, Weaknesses, Opportunities, and Threats) analysis. Make sure that you take some time to add in generational issues here. They will almost always surface in the Opportunities and Threats areas. If you deal successfully with the generational Threat or

Opportunity in *this* planning cycle, you may well have a Strength to laud next cycle.

Finally, whatever kind of planning you are doing—strategic, marketing, financial, or technology—all plans should have goals and objectives, and at least a few of those goals and objectives should be focused on generational issues.

> **HANDS ON**: If you find that the Boomers or GenX or Gen@ are going to be an increasing percentage of your service recipients, a goal in your strategic plan could be something like this:
>
> *Prepare for a 25% increase in GenX users in the next five years.*

> **HANDS ON**: Here are some other generic generation-related goals that may help guide your planning.

- Increase the information available on our website to include much more detailed information for service recipients, volunteers, staff, board, and donors.

- Reevaluate our fringe benefits, work rules, dress code, and family policies to better align them with our workforce.

- Evaluate the retirement plans of our management team and establish a management transition plan if needed.

- Increase our efforts in leadership development to include younger managers and line staff who have interest in becoming managers.

- Develop a program to reduce the average age of our board of directors in the next three years.

- Develop volunteer recruitment programs focused on college and postcollege age volunteers

- Evaluate the effect of boomer retirement and moving on our development efforts.

- Increase our efforts to receive donations online.

Remember to have your planning team generationally representative, particularly for those generations who are a particular focus. If you are planning to meet the needs of the GenX users, for example, you need to have some GenX members on the planning team, and ask a lot of GenX users about what it is they really want.

Mentor and discuss among generations

In Chapter 4, we talked about having mentoring and discussion groups among staff to prevent or resolve intergenerational conflicts and stress. These groups have a second effect: reducing stress and conflicts between staff and the people you serve. If your client base is Gen@ and your service providers are Boomers, or if the reverse is the case, there are always frustrations that pop up. They may seem like simple personality differences, but often it is that one generation's habits or perspectives vex another generation.

Obviously, this can lead to a reduction in customer satisfaction and a con-comitant loss in staff morale. So, get ahead of the curve and expand the subject matter of your intergenerational groups to include discussions about people you serve of different generations.

Target market by generation

We'll talk at length about generational marketing in the next chapter, but remember that people feel they fit with people of their own gender, income level, ethnicity, race, and age. We slice and group ourselves mentally in a lot of ways. While age is most important when we are kids (think high school when freshman don't talk to juniors, and it's a rare senior who would strike up a conversation with a sophomore), it still matters as we get older. My grad-uate students are happy to talk to me or to sit in the commons before or after class to talk about issues surrounding class, politics, or the university. Why are they willing to do that? Because I'm their professor. But they would never invite me out to a bar; they want to hang out with people their own age.

Same for your service recipients. On your web site and in your paper mate-rials, you need pictures of people of the age (and gender and ethnicity) that you are trying to target. Why do you think you see actors with grey hair on TV ads for retirement communities? Or actors with no grey hair in ads for

Viagra? Because the marketers are trying to make age associations, to make you feel that you are part of the group. You need to do the same.

Age down

You have to work your way back down the age curve to predict the *changes in service wants that you need to prepare for.* For example, if your organization is a senior service center, and you are now serving mostly Greatest and Silent Generation members, a train full of Boomers is headed down the track toward you, with different wants, different likes, and a whole lot more people. Even if you don't serve Boomers now, you need to begin understanding them and getting ready for them now.

The basic idea of aging down in the area of services is to predict what's coming in two, five, or ten years.

There are, however exceptions to the rule. While I urge you to age down, in some cases, you have to age up! For example, if you serve mothers and infants and toddlers, twenty years ago you would be mostly serving people in their late teens and twenties. Not now. Thousands of new mothers in their late thirties and well into their forties are out there. This requires a major adjustment in service outlook, sensitivity, and even equipment.

> **FOR EXAMPLE**: I worked with a group of co-op preschool managers within the past year. (In co-ops, the teachers work alongside parents in the classroom.) I asked them what changes they were seeing in their organization. One of the answers to my questions surprised me: "Low stools. We see more (or need more) low stools." Why? Because the parents are predominately in their late thirties and forties and can't easily get up from sitting on the floor, but can from a low stool. Now there's a generational accommodation!

Meet techspectations

Use your generational estimates to examine your technology. If you tend to serve more people of Boomer and older generations, think about things like your web site, your automated answering system, your paper marketing materials. How should they change? Do you need more pictures that eration specific? More white space, a bigger typeface?

> **FOR EXAMPLE**: My book club discussion groups are compo nonprofit executives, and thus, most are Boomers. The grou done by conference call, and each month we begin our review book we've read by giving our overall impression of it—the writing, the topic, and the benefit of the book. I've lost track of the number of times someone has chimed in about a particular book, "I really liked the fact that they used big type! I could still read it late in the evening when my eyes are tired!"

> Think about it—their impression of the book was influenced by the typeface size. Hmmm . . . will their impression of *your* organization be influenced by the typeface size in your written material? Should you stop trying to cram in so much text? Perhaps yes, if your median service age is forty-five or older.

On the other hand, if your service recipients are younger, meet their tech-spectations by having everything about your organization on your web site. *Everything.*

What else? What about educational materials that they can use on their iPods? What about downloadable podcasts? What about ticket sales or scheduling online? Talk to your younger service recipients about what they want.

Ask

Never assume you understand your markets. No matter how much you already know (a lot if you've been at your job for some time), you have to ask. Create what I term a *culture of asking.*

> **HANDS ON**: Talk to your staff about this. The final words that everyone inside your organization needs to say to the people you serve as they leave are, "How was everything today? Is there anything else we could have done for you? Any suggestions?" And *everyone* needs to ask, even if they are not in direct service. People need to know you care.

FOR EXAMPLE: About ten months ago, I was doing a training gig for a group of nonprofit execs at a hotel in Houston. The training room was far too cold, so I called the front desk to get the temperature changed. The maintenance guy showed up quickly, adjusted the temperature, gave me his card, and told me to call if I needed the room colder or warmer as the day progressed.

Then he asked, "Are you a guest in the hotel?" I told him that I was. "Everything in your room OK? If there is *any* problem, call me directly and I'll get it fixed while you are here. Don't wait until you get back to your room!"

I was impressed. This guy got it.

Then the audio-visual guy showed up, checking on my AV status. After I assured him that everything was good, he handed me his card, told me to call if there were any problems. And then he asked, "Are you a guest in the hotel?" Again, I said I was. "Everything in your room OK? If there is any problem, call me directly, and I'll talk to maintenance and get it fixed."

Now I was *really* impressed. Not only did these guys get it, the hotel got it.

Since that time, this sequence of questions has happened to me in three hotels, at different chains. Apparently, the hotel industry is getting very good training on the issue of customer service.

Ask, ask, ask . . . and listen.

Summary

In this chapter, we've examined the all-important issue of the people you serve. These people, as we saw, are also going through a generation change. Just as with your staff, they are Boomers, GenXers, and Gen@s, and if not directly receiving service, then in the families of those who do. Generational sensitivity is crucial in service provision.

To examine this in more detail, we first looked at our four big trends to see how this would play out for you. Then, we turned to your service recipients and what they will look like, including some tools to evaluate how your service recipients look now and how they will look in ten years. What did you see in terms of your need to plan ahead?

Third, we looked at service reconfiguration in light of your service needs assessment. Most service accommodations involve small changes made daily, rather than one-time seismic changes. We looked at some examples of how to do this in a generationally accommodating way.

Finally, we reviewed the Six Big Actions and how they apply to your service recipients.

So, we've examined the trends that will effect your organization, your staff, your board and volunteers, and now, in this chapter, your service recipients. Next, we'll take a look at marketing.

CHAPTER SIX DISCUSSION QUESTIONS

1. How do our services break out generationally? Do we collect adequate information to know, or do we need to estimate?

2. What's happening in the population in our community? Is our community (or our constituency) aging quickly, getting younger, trading generations?

3. What do our service recipients tell us about ways we can improve? Is there an age component to these suggestions?

4. Are we asking our customers what they want often enough? Too often? Are we asking in enough different ways? Are we really listening to what they are telling us? How can we connect better?

5. Are there "hidden" customers whose age is changing? For example, the parents in the co-op preschool who needed stools?

7

Marketing to Generations

MARKETING IS A KEY PART of any successful nonprofit manager's skill set. We need to market to funders, the community, the people we serve, our board, and our staff. So it makes sense to look at the skill of marketing in relation to generations. We want people of all ages to use our services, to donate their time, talent, and treasure to us, and to work with us as we provide mission to our community.

Are the basic principles of marketing the same for different generations? Yes. Do we use the same techniques in the same ways for different generations? Absolutely not. In the following pages, we'll see what generations mean to marketing. First, we'll review the marketing cycle—a sequence of actions that will ensure you are starting off from the correct foundation.

Next, we'll again look at the Four Impacts. Then we'll focus on the phenomenon of MeBranding, which has major marketing implications and is crucial to your success over the next ten years. After we've wrestled with MeBranding, we'll turn to some specific technology help you can get in your marketing efforts.

Finally, we'll once again go through the Six Big Actions and how to adapt them to your marketing efforts. By the end of the chapter, you'll know how to reach out to each of the key generations that are influencing your organization.

A Quick Review of the Marketing Cycle

The marketing cycle outlined here works whether you are marketing to clients, staff, board, or funders. It is applicable to both new and existing services. It works for Gen@ and Greatest Generation members and every generation in between.

Marketing is a cycle of never-ending inquiry, adaptation, accommodation, promotion, and evaluation. You can't do marketing just once and succeed. It's an endless task. And there's a key truth about it that you ignore to your great peril:

Everything everyone in your organization does every day is marketing.

This is as true for services as it is for recruitment and retention, as important for twenty-somethings as it is for the over-seventy set. Everything, every day, every place.

There are seven steps in the cycle:

1. Identify your market
2. Find out what your market wants
3. Develop or amend your service or product
4. Set a reasonable price
5. Promote and deliver the service or product
6. Evaluate
7. Start over

The following review explores these steps in the context of generational change, even though they are applicable much more broadly.

1. Identify your market

First things first—who are you marketing to? Different markets often need to be accommodated in different ways. Identifying your market is often hard, and always worth the effort, because it allows you to focus more on a specific market's wants rather than just generalize for everyone. In generational terms, of course, market segmentation will come in the form of age groups. We need to drill down through all of our services to identify which age groups we are serving. An analysis for a symphony orchestra follows.

Note: The terms *Primary, Secondary,* and *Tertiary* refer to weight of the target market. Thus the primary market for any part of the organization is the most important.

Classical Symphony Series:

Primary: Boomer

Secondary: Silent Generation

Tertiary: GenX

Pops Series:

Primary: Boomer

Secondary: GenX

Tertiary: Gen@

Development:

Primary: Silent Generation

Secondary: Boomer

Tertiary: GenX

Caution: Don't interpret primary, secondary and tertiary as having equal value. For example, the development markets might be Silent Generation, 70 percent; Boomer, 25 percent; and GenX, 5 percent.

Note that this organization is heavily weighted toward older patrons. While this is not unusual for classical music organizations, it should be a wake-up call for the board and staff in their strategic planning.

2. Find out what your market wants

Nonprofits regularly make the mistake of assuming that people will seek what they need. We are good at needs analysis, needs assessment, diagnosis, and the like (which is unarguably essential to our work). However, this often infects our marketing with the attitude that "if we build it they will come." That assumption is flawed. Do communities need the arts? Of course. Then why are the arts always underfunded? Do people need to live healthy lifestyles? Of course. Then why are we in the United States the most obese nation in history? Do we each *need* to have an SUV? Of course not, but we're still a nation of SUV drivers.

While we all have *needs,* we all seek *wants.* In marketing our services, our jobs, or our volunteer opportunities, we need to know what people want if we are to be successful. To do that, we have to be willing to ask. Wants (and concomitant value) are defined by the market, not by you. Just because you know someone needs something—that it would be good for them—does not translate into their wanting it. The user perspective is key.

I refer the nonprofit tendency to market to needs instead of wants as a *marketing disability.* Effective nonprofits know how to convert their needs assessments into *wants* assessments. For-profit marketers are expert at this, seeking to make people want stuff they don't need. Meanwhile, we nonprofit marketers should try to make people want stuff they *do* need.

> **FOR EXAMPLE:** Consider alcohol abuse. Back in the 1960s the federal government funded a huge increase in alcohol (and later drug) treatment beds, based on research that showed the prevalence of alcoholism demanded them, and the concomitant premise that the availability of treatment (often free) would fill the beds quickly and address the problem on a national scale.
>
> In other words, they built it, and expected people in need to come. Of course, if you have been through Alcoholics Anonymous or know someone who has, you know the difficult truth: people in need want care *a whole lot later* than when they first need it. Everyone around them knows they need it, and they still don't seek help immediately, often delaying until a true crisis shakes them up.

There are significantly fewer treatment beds now than forty years ago (adjusted for population) and they still aren't full. One reasons for the decrease in treatment beds is this needs-versus-wants issue.

So, to make people want what they *do* need, professionals in alcohol and drug prevention and treatment are constantly looking for new ways to encourage addicts to seek and, equally important, stay in, treatment. The professionals have realized that wants rule.

3. Develop or amend your service or product

We devoted the last chapter to this particular phase of the marketing cycle: how target markets (in this case, generations) shape your service provision. Once you know what your various markets want, you can begin to develop (or more often, amend and improve) your services or products. As noted previously, this rarely means wholesale change. Small, constant improvements around the edges of a service or product can make all the difference for consumers—and for consumers of all ages.

> **FOR EXAMPLE**: A visual arts organization in the far West used this technique to improve its relationship with a key generation. The management team (all older Boomers) had been joking with each other about their increasing difficulty both to clearly see small print and read in low-light environments (very, very common facts of life for those of us over fifty). Years before, they had switched to nine- and ten-point fonts (from the more common twelve-point) for their marketing material as well as the handouts that patrons received to provide background information on the art in each new showing. The organization did this as a way of saving space and paper. So, after joking about age and optics, someone asked, because most of their patrons were over fifty, whether they should consider going back to the larger font. They did, and started printing their management reports in larger fonts. Everyone on the management team was happier, and the organization received numerous comments from patrons, who also noticed the difference it made.

Other little improvements—like putting all your policies online (for Gen@), establishing flex time (for GenX and Gen@), or standardizing a dress code (for Boomers)—can make a huge difference, even if they are so subtle no one "notices."

4. Set a reasonable price

There are two truths about nonprofit pricing:

Nonprofits are trained to underprice. Whether it be from accommodating matching funds, or listening to people who say "You're a nonprofit, you ought to give things away," or from (in many cases) serving people who don't have much money, nonprofits nearly universally prefer to price low when they have control over their prices at all. Resist that urge. Why? Because of the second truth:

It's never about price—it's always about value. We tend to think that low cost wins. Look at Wal-Mart (and for the moment, set aside the company's politics). But Wal-Mart is not just about low cost. It's about *huge selection of comparable products at lowest cost.* What Wal-Mart is saying is this: if you come to Wal-Mart, you can choose among many products, nearly all of which are identical to those at other stores, with one exception: cost.

> **HANDS ON:** Generational considerations in price sometimes overwhelm personal financial situations. The most commonly accepted generational stereotype in this area is for members of the Greatest Generation: these people lived through the searing experience of the Great Depression and have never, ever forgotten it. Thus, when pricing things for this generation, note that their income level is not necessarily a direct indicator of their willingness to be parted from their money.
>
> Similarly, generational concerns arise with the twenty-something Gen@ workers, most of whom have significant debt from their undergraduate or graduate studies. Thus, a twenty-five-year old tech worker whose salary is $90,000 may have less free cash than you think for, say, tickets to your concert series, if he or she is servicing a $75,000 college loan.

People value your services for many reasons. To find out why—why they return, why board members come to meetings, why staff stay more than a year, why annual donors donate every year—you have to ask questions that help you determine what value you are giving them. Armed with that information, you can begin to set a price that reflects the value, your costs of provision, and your goals for that particular service's return to your organization. (Whether it operates at a loss, breaks even, or generates a surplus depends on your goals.)

5. Promote and deliver the service or product

Many people think marketing starts and ends with promotion, public relations, and sales. Only after you do all the earlier steps in the cycle can you do these two key things: deliver the service (where, when, and how the market wants) and tell them about it (where, when, and how they will best hear about it). In terms of generational management this has huge implications. MeBranding says deliver the services in an individually tailored manner—which is, of course, expensive. Can you accommodate that? Gen@ wants to know and learn about everything online, while the Silent Generation wants paper. You may need to provide information in various media—or you may need to focus your promotion on the method that best reaches your primary audience. It all depends, of course, on the service you are promoting.

The key mistake people make in this area is promoting before they ask. And if they do ask, they fail to listen.

6. Evaluate

What worked? What didn't? After all your asking and accommodating, were people happier with you? Did customers return? Did staff turnover lessen? Are donations up? If so, terrific, but there's always room for improvement.

7. Start over

Just like a wheel on a moving car, one full rotation just leads to another. Why should you want to start over? Didn't you already figure out who you were serving and what they wanted, adapt to those wants, and get the service priced, promoted and delivered? Of course, but here's the key: time has passed. Things are different now. So you must keep asking, keep accommodating, and keep meeting those wants.

Now that we've reviewed what marketing is about (at a basic level), let's turn to focus on the Four Impacts and how they affect generation-specific marketing.

The Four Impacts and Marketing

Now let's take a few pages and walk through the Four Impacts and see how they affect marketing and, more importantly, how your marketing efforts can affect them.

Boomers coming in the door

One key market for you is Boomers as potential employees. You certainly want to make good use of the resource of highly experienced, mature potential employees coming to you after their first career is done. You can't afford to be inflexible as you recruit and retain staff: the world wants more flexibility and customization (to the point of MeBranding, which we'll cover in the next section). On the other hand, you need to focus on what these potential boomer employees want.

> **HANDS ON:** In the chapter on staffing, we found that many potential Boomer employees are looking for part-time work to supplement their income, but also to provide for health care benefits. In our opening discussion of different generations, what did we see Boomers wanted? *A cause.* Thus, it would make sense to promote not only your higher mission, but also your flexibility in work hours and your benefits.

Of course, Boomers are also a great source of customers—and there are a *lot* of Boomers out there. Do you want them to be a target market for your services? It may not be that you provide services *to* them, but rather that they are the *decision makers* for services for their children or grandchildren (or aging parents).

> **FOR EXAMPLE**: If you run a youth activity program for toddlers, be aware of how many of the children are being brought in by young mothers and how many are being brought in by *grandmothers* (who will increasingly be Boomers). Is there a different way to appeal to them, to make the decision to come to your activities? If you are a symphony and have a youth concert series, think about targeting a grandparent/grandchild focus. Grandparents (Boomers) will be more likely to have the time, the money, and the interest in passing on their love of classical music to their grandchildren.

> **HANDS ON**: For direct customers, return again to the list of things Boomers want: lifelong learning, a cause, and staying forever young. So, can you redesign your marketing materials to emphasize the "youthful" aspects of your programs (without appearing to be only for young people), the learning that will occur, and the dedication to a higher cause? If so, you'll attract Boomers.

Boomers going out the door

Now let's examine the reverse problem: Boomers going out the door. Is this just a problem or is this an opportunity? It's an opportunity, if you remember a few things. First, you need to talk to your Boomers *before* or at least *as* they ponder retirement, not after they have announced their plans. These discussions can have two effects: you lessen surprises (from people you assumed were going to stay but instead intend to take the first available train out of town), and you get an opportunity to inform them that retirement is not the only option. What information can you give them? For those you want to keep (and this is a key part of the *opportunity* side of this trend), tell them that you hope they will stay, and find out what they are looking for.

FOR EXAMPLE: The CEO of a midsize nonprofit in Texas responded to an issue of my online newsletter recently describing their Boomer retention policy. The CEO had run the numbers and found that 50 percent of her management team was over fifty-five. Rather than trying to keep them all on full time, she had listed the staff, decided who she would really like to keep and who she would not miss quite as much. She had looked at each manager's direct reports and projected who in that group could move up and who would probably not. She also assessed the full skill set of the Boomers to evaluate whether they could fill other roles part-time.

After doing this assessment, she went to the Boomers she wanted to retain and asked them what their plans were and whether they had considered going part-time or even becoming a consultant to the organization. The results? I'll let the CEO describe them:

"The people I talked to were flattered I had visited them and asked them to stay. Of the fourteen people I met with, all told me their plans, and I was surprised at the range of responses. Some were hoping to die with their boots on, some were planning to leave much earlier than I expected. This gave me ample warning. Three of the managers had never considered working part-time or consulting, and all of them opted for that role and are already providing major benefits to the organization, because we could use their skills in an area that they love and have great talent in, but where we don't need a full-time person on their level. A couple of managers just wanted benefits, so we figured out how to do that by letting them cut back, but still keep their health care.

"And the managers I didn't talk to about staying got the message. Of the five in that group, four have left, making room for some much-needed advancement of people junior to them. For me, for the Boomers, and for our organization, this early discussion was a win-win-win."

So, remember to evaluate and ask early. And, keep in mind that this technique does not just apply to managers. It has just as much benefit for line staff. Start and keep that dialogue going.

Also, remember a suggestion I made in our staff chapter: ask people as they leave why they are leaving, what can be done to improve the organization, and what might have caused them to stay longer. This is crucial information for you, and is often much more objective than from people who may be concerned about retaliation if they "tell it like it is."

Whatever happened to GenX and Gen@?

You may well be targeting GenX and Gen@ members already for services, to be employees, or to volunteer. But as you market to them for any or all of these roles, remember a couple of things.

First, particularly for Gen@, but more and more so for GenX, people in these groups are online all the time. You need to meet them where they are, and where they are is online. Thus, any and all information you want them to see needs to be first and foremost on your web site, and you need to be comfortable with the fact that your primary method of communication with them will be e-mail.

> **HANDS ON**: Prepare your technology and your staff to check e-mail more regularly than they may be used to. I still work with nonprofit staff who only check their e-mail once every few days. In today's market, that is absolutely unacceptable. While I understand that e-mail can be a huge black hole for time, remember my story about the Gen@ staff member who e-mailed, left two voice messages, and then came down the hall, all in the space of a half hour or so. You have to respond quickly.

Additionally, you have to be able to work all the media outlets to appeal to the various needs of the GenX and Gen@ communities. What do they want? Well, we learned in the staffing and customer chapters that these generations lean toward believing the reviews of peers, and they like to be and work in groups. So, how do you use those wants in your marketing? What about a reviews section of your web site that notes volunteer experiences, or staff feelings about working, or customer reviews about the value of your mission? What about a blog from staff that notes the high points (and perhaps even frustrations) of trying to serve a community with too few resources? What about setting up group discussion sites for volunteers, or employees, or board members?

All of these techniques combine the GenX and Gen@ expectation for technology with avenues of marketing that appeal to them and make them feel more comfortable with you, whether your goal is to get some of their time, or their talent, or their treasure.

> **FOR EXAMPLE**: A nonprofit in organization located in the Midwest runs many of its programs using volunteers. They had a creative idea (actually innovative and unusual at the time they did it) of starting a discussion blog just for volunteers. Access to the blog is in the organization's volunteer-specific area of their web site. To go online and add to the discussion, you need to register your name and e-mail address. Once the blog was set up, they "seeded" it with a few postings solicited from current volunteers. Then they e-mailed their entire volunteer list and told volunteers directly about it at events.

> The results? "Amazing, in a number of ways," said the organization's CEO. First, new volunteers rose by 15 percent more than in any six-month period in their history—and every one of the volunteers was thirty-five or younger. Second, they got especially good feedback on the volunteer experience, both at their organization, and, interestingly, at other local organizations. People from all over the world (really) jumped into the discussion and told about their volunteer horror stories, what satisfied them, what brought them back. "We had to learn fast, and adapt quickly, but having this kind of feedback in nearly real time has paid off handsomely."

Unintended consequences

The most common unintended consequence in the discipline of marketing occurs when you have a "set it and forget it" mind-set. Many organizations go through the marketing planning process, develop the plan, ask their constituents lots of questions, and then assume that the plan and information will carry them through for thirty-six months.

The unintended consequence is that the plan and information goes out of date with lightning speed. Thus our need to innovate in marketing constantly, just as in providing services. The technology we use today will be outdated before we know it.

FOR EXAMPLE: At this writing, my daughter Caitlin has just turned eighteen. As a high school senior, she is an avid user of text messages on her phone and of instant messaging (IM) on her computer. I often come downstairs to our house computer to find her carrying on IM conversations with ten friends while also talking on her cell phone.

On a recent trip, we were talking about one of her projects for student council, and I suggested that she e-mail her friends later that day to get some feedback. Her response: "None of my friends really ever use their e-mail, Dad." (The "Dad" was said with enough irony to suggest that I was ninety-five years old and totally out of touch with reality.) I was incredulous. "You don't use e-mail . . . you? You grew up using e-mail," I protested.

"Dad! No one e-mails. We just text." And she proceeded to text a five- or six-sentence message to ten friends in about a minute and a half while we were driving down the road. Flying thumbs.

"Done. They'll get back to me soon."

A marketing plan that relied on e-mail as a promotional technique to reach Caitlin's age group—say a plan made three years earlier, when text messaging was too new to show up on the radar—*would completely miss the boat* on reaching Caitlin and her friends. That same marketing plan done today would discard e-mail in favor of cell phones, because that's where the market is. Since technology is changing so rapidly—and it is a key to reaching your audiences—you're going to need to update and evaluate your marketing continuously.

Unintended consequences often just happen. But more often, they occur when we aren't paying close attention to our surroundings. With change cycles accelerating, we need to be really, really on top of things to not waste precious resources marketing in ways that no one is paying attention to.

So, there are the Four Impacts and how they affect marketing. Now let's take some time attending to an issue that may well overwhelm everything else we do in marketing: MeBranding.

MeBranding

In generational marketing, there is no larger issue than what I earlier labeled MeBranding (see Chapter 2 for a complete discussion). To recap, MeBranding is the customization of products and services down to the smallest possible denominator: the individual. Think of it as the old Burger King slogan "Have it your way!" writ large. MeBranding is a marketing strategy that has morphed into a consumer expectation that crosses generations, though weighted more heavily the younger you go. The unintended consequence of MeBranding is that consumers (your clients and constituents) are frustrated when you don't give them what they want, when they want it.

In some ways—at least when it comes to the ways we think of our volunteers and our staff, this "me-centeredness" flies in the face of nonprofit culture: It's not about what "I" want, it's about helping others. And even when it is the "others" we're trying to serve, we run on such tight budgets that ultracustomization seems beyond possibility.

But MeBranding is here to stay. It is an extension of the fact that marketing in nonprofits is about meeting people's needs in a way that they want, and here's the key: what individuals increasingly want is not to be a part of a market, but to be the market.

Let's look at how this can play out in five parts of your organization, organized from internal audiences (employees and volunteers) to external audiences. These five are staff benefits, volunteers, donor attraction and retention, service design, and service scheduling.

MeBenefits

Here's a great place to start. Benefits are a crucial part of the expectations of most employees, whether full-time or part-time—and employees are one of your key markets. Benefits are also a place where we can compete against other employers if we really drill down and find out what's important to each employee, and then work toward being as flexible as possible.

For most employers (and I hope you are in this group) the first thing that springs to mind is flexible benefits where each employee sets aside a portion of their pay (as tax-free payroll deductions) to be spent on predicted health expenses through the coming year. Check with your accountant or trade association about how this works in your state. There are downsides to it, but in general it's a win-win.

Your nonprofit can also offer MeBenefits by setting up a menu of options allowing each employee to target your contribution toward what they most need (subject to federal, state, and local regulations, of course). For example, some nonprofits set a personal amount for benefits per employee. The employee then chooses between options, such as a high or low personal contribution to a health care plan, perhaps using the remainder for a fitness club. Of course, the more employees you have, the easier it is to get your insurer to give you options. Talk to your state trade association about insurance and benefit options that they may be pursuing.

Other paid benefits might include reimbursing people for taking public transportation, or giving people paid time off to volunteer in groups on designated days.

You can also look at other, nonmonetary benefits. Should you allow people to come in whenever, or set strict working hours? Can people work from home some or all of the time? Can they take time off for personal reasons? How much? Does vacation time accrue, or do they need to use it or lose it? Whatever your policy, make sure your management team does not reverse the benefits of a flexible policy by putting pressure on staff to not take time off, or making them feel guilty about not being at work 24/7.

Never assume you know what your staff want. Ask them. You can survey about this, but you'll probably get more useful information from a series of focus groups.

MeVolunteering

Customization is a particularly important and vexing issue for younger volunteers, who tend to want to volunteer in groups, don't want you to waste their time, and want to work only the time *they* have available, not necessarily when you need them. Of course, you can't have Habitat for Humanity build in one-hour increments spread over a month. But, if your target group is younger, more options and more flexibility here is probably something that they will appreciate and, more importantly, flock to.

MeDonations

This seems pretty straightforward—a set of different amounts to give ($5, $25, $100, $500), and a few different ways to pay (check, cash, credit card or PayPal). But it's not that simple.

The most popular option at the United Way is targeted donations, and this is cascading into direct giving at individual nonprofits (often with the un-welcome corollary of not wanting the donor's money to be used for administrative costs). But more and more donors want individual reports on what happened with their money, and many large donors are seeking to be more involved (or looking over your shoulder—it's a matter of perspective). Some donors want visibility; some anonymity. Some want rewards (like a certificate or plaque); some abhor the thought of money being spent on trophies rather than mission.

> **FOR EXAMPLE:** In 1990, when my consulting firm had twelve employees, we got a visit from the United Way volunteer for our area, looking to encourage me to have an employee fund drive. I took the forms they offered, and at our next staff meeting, handed them out, noting that no one was under any pressure to contribute through our firm, but that they did have the option to target their donation to one or more specific nonprofits. I told them the firm would match the first

$100 they gave, and that they could target the entire amount. I had great employees, and they all donated. So far, so good.

Then the United Way volunteer returned to pick up the donation forms. As he reviewed the forms I told him that we had 100 percent participation, and handed him the firm's matching check. Was he happy? No. He frowned as he reviewed the forms. He looked up and said. "Uh, we really aren't encouraging donors to target their donations. . . . uh. . . . I mean . . . it is an option, but. . . . well, all your employees took that option . . . and if *everyone* did that, what would our Allocation Committee have to do?"

Three of my fellow employees were in the room as the volunteer said this and they slowly turned to look at me to see what I'd say.

"We've made our choices and, despite what the United Way may think, it's *our* money, and *our* decision. You can take the money with the designation, or we can keep it and write checks directly to the organizations ourselves. That's *your* choice." He took the money.

But the story didn't end there. About three months later, the annual fund drive was over. The same volunteer showed up one day with two huge, very fancy plaques for us, one for being a 100 percent participating agency, and one for me for being a United Way Leader or Pathfinder or something that meant as the boss, I was, I suppose, a great humanitarian. These were big, expensive plaques, I knew, as I had once purchased similar ones.

I was incensed. I asked the United Way volunteer, "How much do you think these cost?" Not waiting for an answer, I continued, "I'll tell you how much they cost, they cost more than the entire annual donation of at least two of our hard-working employees, people who don't really have that money to spare, but who gave it out of the goodness of their hearts and who now will see these obscene awards as a waste of their money."

The volunteer was dumbfounded. "But everyone loves the awards . . ." he said, meekly.

"Not me," I said. "We didn't *give* a donation to *get* anything, and certainly not a piece of mahogany and brass. Awards like this are flat-out insulting. Take them with you and don't even think about asking us for a donation next year."

I've told that story probably one hundred times to audiences over the years, and people always (every single time) come up with similar stories of clueless fundraisers from all types of organizations who were out of touch with what they wanted as donors. Think, ask, listen, and be flexible.

MeServices

MeServices are counterintuitive to most nonprofit management teams. They tell me, "We need to scale what we do, hit the sweet spot of where most people want services, and do lots of that." I understand. This is "bell-curve" thinking. In almost any traditional bell curve the majority of people are in the middle, and those are the people you want to focus on to meet the most wants.

True in the past, not so much now. The bell curve has, essentially flattened as the culture has embraced what technology has enabled: individualized services. I am not assuming that you can afford to provide completely individualized services for every person who walks in the door; for many organizations that's unaffordable. But this doesn't mean that we can't make services feel more individual.

> **FOR EXAMPLE**: Take a cue from great salespeople and politicians: call patrons by name. Being welcomed by name is a huge positive for most people, even if you pronounce their name wrong. A friend told me of an encounter with a new physician's receptionist. The clinic had started a policy where patients were offered the opportunity to have their pictures taken (just a headshot). It was explained to the patients that the pictures would be kept with their file and used to help the

staff remember patients. The reception staff regularly reviewed the files of patients who were due in the next hour or two, and greeted them by name as they walked in the door. The names of the patients were spelled phonetically on the picture so that pronunciation was correct (mostly). In addition, instead of a nurse coming to the door to the waiting room and calling out a name like a cattle call, he or she could look at the picture, go over to the patient and greet them.

My friend, after being greeted by name, asked the receptionist what the reaction of the other patients was. She said that about half had not wanted their picture taken initially, but when they arrived for their next visit and saw others being greeted by name, many asked to be photographed! This is a small, simple, and inexpensive method of customization, and people love it.

MeServices might include e-mail reminders of appointments (for Boomers) or text message reminders (for Gen@ members) or the ability to pay online instead of in person, or having more time options for services (taking a cue from day care nonprofits, some of which are open twenty hours a day).

These options don't have to be complex, lengthy, or expensive. For many nonprofits, just offering *some* choice will be enough.

Imagine you are in a restaurant (the only one you've ever eaten in), and the menu has one item, served one way. And, you *have* to eat there. One day you walk in and there are three choices. Imagine the improvement in your opinion of the restaurant. Note the example doesn't say, "One day there are three *hundred* choices." Give people options and let them choose. That's a great start on MeBranding.

Sit down with users of your services to see whether there are things they would like to have customizable. As a benefit, you'll hear about general improvement needs as well.

MeScheduling

Working hours for employees, volunteering times for service volunteers, the times of board meetings, the frequency of staff meetings, the hours you are "open," the hours you are available to respond to service requests, the availability of information when a client wants it—these are all examples of MeScheduling.

> **HANDS ON**: If you have appointments for services, or sell tickets, or have a calendar of events, put it online. Put it *all* online. Make sure it is always up to date. Let people set appointments, purchase tickets, and see what's going on through your web site. It is the fastest, easiest way to meet people on their schedule.

Reexamine the actual hours you are open in relation to your target generations. Is there a benefit to extended hours on certain days? Or to simply adjusting your availability, being open fewer hours on one day and more on another? Ask your markets and find out what schedule meets their needs.

There is a downside to offering so many choices: it is expensive, and can confuse and frustrate people, particularly Boomers like me. And this can stymie purchase decisions.

> **HANDS ON**: Which choices to offer should come from asking, not assuming. Ask your target constituents which choices appeal to them. If you are exploring benefit options, ask staff what they think—you can even ask people you'd eventually like to attract to your organization. If you are looking at ways to donate or ways to celebrate and recognize donors, ask existing donors—and potential donors—what options appeal to them.

Marketing to a MeBranded society is about staying in touch, being flexible, and offering a reasonable number of choices and options. Work with your staff, board, and funders to make sure you can maintain sufficient flexibility to meet the wants of an increasingly individualized community.

Technology and Marketing to Generations

While we'll spend the entirety of Chapter 8 on technology, the intersection of marketing and tech is key. Here are some things to consider.

Adapt technology to fit the generation you're marketing to

Just as the generations are different in their attitudes, background, and perceptions of the world, so do they differ in their use of technology. In general, the younger the audience, the more comfortable they are with technology—and the more adept you need to be in your use of it when marketing.

Because different generations look at technology differently, make sure that after you identify your target markets (for customers, donors, employees, and volunteers) you adapt your use of technology to attract and retain them from a generational viewpoint.

> **FOR EXAMPLE**: One Midwest agency now has its quarterly newsletter in two versions—paper and electronic—and it delivers it via three modes: U.S. Post, e-mail, and web, as the customer wishes. Not surprisingly, the agency has found that most of the Gen@ and GenX employees and volunteers view the newsletter online—but not all. About 10 percent prefer paper. For Boomers, it's about 50–50. And about 80 percent of their Silent and Greatest Generation supporters want paper. The key to this example is that the user has the choice!

> **FOR EXAMPLE**: An organization based in a Great Plains college town started a blog in late 2004, written by a twenty-three-year-old volunteer about his volunteer experiences. The idea was to engage younger volunteers. It worked. The blogger got 440 comments, responses, and e-mails in his *first week* online. The organization immediately tried expanding the idea to Boomers who were potential donors, using a Boomer blogger volunteer who focused on the value of the mission

and the options for donations. Nobody read the blog. Was it the age, the subject, or the blogger? The organization never found out, but was smart enough to stop doing something that didn't work.

FOR EXAMPLE: A Florida nonprofit executive was surprised when her senior volunteers asked her to put pictures of the volunteer activities online. She asked the volunteers (most of whom were octogenarians) why they wanted the pictures online when they were posted on the bulletin board and in the paper newsletter. Did they want to view the pictures at home? "Oh, no!" they chuckled. "We don't need to see them there. We just want them online and to have the Internet address so that our children and grandchildren can see them!"

In each of these examples, the organization tried to be sensitive to different levels of tech comfort, tech savvy, and tech lure. Most important, they assumed nothing, as illustrated in the examples of the 10 percent of young people who prefer paper, and the senior citizens who wanted online photos. Rather, they matched the marketing approach to fit the desires of their target audience.

Use technology to improve access

As a marketer, you want to be available and accessible to the widest range of people in ways that solve their problems and get them interested in your organization. Your web site is the most obvious area in which technology can dramatically improve access. We'll talk more about web sites in Chapter 8, but suffice it to say here that your site needs to be easy to understand and navigate, have different areas for different groups, have information on your mission or cause, and be easy to read for people with all ranges of eyesight. In addition, the site has to answer questions from return visitors, from regular users, from staff, board, donors, and so forth. (An executive recently described her web site as an unsupervised tour of her organization. She tries to imagine what a new visitor would want to see and puts it on the site.)

Another area where technology helps improve access is with low-cost word processing and printing. This means that paper materials can be easily produced in-house, and in low volume, so that you can develop many brochures rather than just one, with each targeted to a particular market.

E-mail and voice mail are a third area of access. Provide e-mail and voice contact information on your web site and all written materials. If you use an automated answering system, include direct extension numbers. Make contacting you as easy as possible. Then, make sure that someone is checking the e-mail and voice mail constantly. One want that is shared by every generation: the desire to have their calls and messages returned promptly.

Caution: In your fervor to be accessible, be reasonable with your staff. One small agency executive decided that his organization would have someone available to return calls 24/7. He was enamored of call forwarding technology, and assigned each staff person in a rotation to be on call to return calls. You might assume that the agency's work was time-critical—perhaps a battered women's shelter, or a service for runaways. Not so. It was a summer camp! The staff resented the need to be near a phone all the time (this was in the days when cell coverage was spotty), and staff morale plummeted.

Use your technology to collect information and answer questions

Another area where tech can help is in putting out information, and allowing you to reach out to ask for help, money, input, opinions. Let's look at how you might use tech to help in this area.

Your web site is a terrific tool to answer lots of questions quickly and efficiently around the clock. Make sure your site is rich with information, intuitive, and that most information can be found in three clicks. More on this in Chapter 8, but remember that these days, your first point of contact is more than likely to be your web site.

HANDS ON: I am flat-out appalled by how many commercial and nonprofit sites seem to be set up to *not* let me find contact information for staff. If I know you, and I have question for you, how many clicks would it take for me to find your direct phone line and or e-mail? Take a look right now. Go to your web site and see. If it's more than three, I'm not a happy camper.

Surveys can often be done very quickly, efficiently, and cost effectively on-line, with an e-mail providing a link to an HTML site. Remember, however, that there are people who don't have access to the Net, or who prefer not to use it, so results are skewed. Less so the younger your target inquiry group is, but still to some degree no matter what generation you are looking at.

E-mail is still the communication method of choice for most people, but remember that instant messaging is growing in use, and fax is still out there, so have the capacity to use all three.

Good marketing facilitates exchanges between your organization and its constituents. It improves the community's opinion of your organization and increases the rate of satisfaction with your services. If you overdepend on technology, or miss what have become standard techspectations—in short, if you don't hit the tech "sweet spot," you risk doing just the reverse of what you intended. People will think you are out of touch, behind the times, or worst of all, *that you don't understand them.* And if they think that, you are in serious trouble.

The Six Big Actions and Marketing

As in prior chapters, let's look at the Six Big Actions and how they can help you in your marketing efforts.

Include generational issues in planning

This entire chapter has covered generational issues with regard to marketing. So here, just a reminder: you should have a marketing plan, and that marketing plan should attend to target audiences. However you break out your current audiences, be sure to incorporate a generational overlay, including an examination of what those markets want, a match-up of those wants with your organization's core competencies, and some goals and objectives to ask and respond to the markets as they evolve. Then be sure that your plan anticipates and addresses likely changes as generations age.

Mentor and discuss among generations

In our previous chapters, we've talked about using mentors from one generation to help others in that generation acclimate to the organization, or be sensitive to a particular generational perspective. Here, my suggestion is much simpler: put members of every generation on your marketing team (you should have one) and make sure that those generational representatives understand that part of their role is to provide generational perspective on such things as asking, promotion, web sites, and so forth.

These representatives also need to be alert to what other members of their generational group are doing, thinking, saying, asking. If generational issues are going to be incorporated effectively into your marketing planning as we discussed above, you need to have both generational representation and active discussion.

Target market by generation

This should be part of your marketing plan. If you are putting a generational filter on your markets as you evaluate them, you may find some surprising information. And that examination may well explain your current situation more accurately than previously.

> **FOR EXAMPLE**: A client organization of mine had a marketing director who attended a statewide session in 2004 on better survey techniques, and returned to her organization excited about the uses of HTML-based surveys through web sites such as SurveyMonkey. She worked up a survey, sent e-mails out to the entire e-mail list, and sat back and waited.

Not much happened. Her e-mail surveys usually garnered a 10–15 percent return rate within two weeks, but the online survey did less than 1 percent. The marketing director, who was in her early thirties, e-mailed me to ask for some advice. After we checked that the survey had, in fact been delivered to recipient's in-boxes, I asked her two questions: What was the age breakout by decade (21–30, 31–40, 41–50, and so on.) of the recipients of the e-mail, and what was the breakout for the written surveys? She had no idea, but said she'd check. Two days later she got back to me. On the written survey, the vast majority of returns had been from people over fifty. The e-mail list was heavily weighted with people over fifty as well, with over half being over sixty. So, a generational look at the respondents revealed the reason for the low returns.

Age down

This action hinges on the fact that up to now, most of your marketing efforts probably focused on Boomers. Start now trending down in terms of age in your focus, your techniques, and your technology in your marketing efforts. Refresh your staff's awareness of the math concept of "median" in your marketing. Your median age should be steadily moving down, no matter what you do, or who your targets are. Even if the ages of your service base, your donor base, and your board are all Boomer or higher, and your median age is thus relatively high, the trend needs to be downward over time.

Meet techspectations

Go where the market is, remembering that different markets have different techspectations. My daughter's generation is on their cell phone, on the web, and instant messaging. My (Boomer) friends use their e-mail (but hate spam), and spend more time on the web, while reading their snail mail less and less. GenX and Gen@ want reviews and online discussions. Everyone (and I do mean *everyone*) hates slogging their way through automated answering systems.

Some members of your community strongly prefer paying their bills, purchasing their concert tickets, making appointments, or making donations online. Some recoil at the thought.

The challenge is to create a mix of these technologies that give the choice to the consumer/user/donor in a manner that is seamless, while not condescending to any one group. And that's not easy.

Ask

Ask, really? Of course, you know this is the key by now. Not only is it a crucial part of the marketing cycle, but I hope that you realize that the asking cycle needs to be constant, not biannual.

Summary

In this chapter we've examined the effect of generational change on your organization. We reviewed the marketing cycle, which is as follows:

1. Identify your market

2. Find out what your market wants

3. Develop or amend your service or product

4. Set a reasonable price

5. Promote and deliver the service or product

6. Evaluate

7. Start over

We visited the Four Impacts, and their specific influence on marketing. I urged you to focus, focus, focus on the different generations, whether the trend in question was Boomers coming in, Boomers going out, or appealing to members of GenX or Gen@.

Then we turned to a huge issue that affects marketing and service delivery—MeBranding. We reviewed five distinct areas where MeBranding can affect your organization. These are

- MeBenefits
- MeVolunteering
- MeDonations
- MeServices
- MeScheduling

Each of these has its own unique set of issues and suggested responses.

We looked at some specific ideas regarding the use of technology in marketing. A quick recap of these ideas follows:

- Adapt technology to fit the generation you're marketing to
- Use tech to improve access
- Use your technology to collect information and answer questions

Finally, we quickly went through the Six Big Actions and marketing. Since many of the actions have their roots in good marketing technique, we did not belabor the points, but focused on one or two reminders in each.

Marketing is a key part of any successful nonprofit manager's skill set. It is the skill that can have the most positive effect on any nonprofit organization, and its careful and focused use is crucial in dealing with generational issues. I hope by this point, you agree.

But there are other issues to explore, and it will surprise no one that we need to spend some time on a growing presence in our society: technology. That's the subject of the next chapter.

CHAPTER SEVEN DISCUSSION QUESTIONS

1. Should we use the marketing cycle to reevaluate our marketing in light of generational change?

2. Do we need to look at our target markets again? Who are they, and do they break out by generation? How? Should we rework our marketing plan?

3. Do we need to reexamine how we get our message across through various technologies to ensure that we are not excluding or turning off any generational group?

4. What about the tech vehicle of our asking? Is it effective, or do we need to plan and implement some changes?

5. Are we really *listening* to every generation, or are we just asking? How can we tell?

6. What are two or three ways we can specifically accommodate to MeBranding? Which market should we look at first?

8

Generations and Technology

"So, what's your iPod policy here? What about IM?"

"How are you integrating mailing lists into your community discussion and information groups?"

"How often do you check out blogs that discuss your organization specifically or your cause in general?"

"Can I donate to your organization online with PayPal?"

If your reaction to any or all of the questions above was "Huh?" then you are going to get a lot out of this chapter. Let's look at some more questions:

"How do I get access to the Internet?"

"I am not comfortable around computers, so can you please mail me information about your services?"

"Why don't you have a real person answer the phone during business hours?"

"I don't have a (don't like) credit card(s) . . . can I write you a check?"

These are tech questions, too, and just as important as the first set.

In this chapter we'll look at technology and its effects on all the generations you touch in your nonprofit organization. We'll examine the techspectations of different generations, and how you can accommodate them. I'll show you simple and complex solutions to tech problems and bring you up to speed on resources for your tech efforts.

We'll begin by looking at the Four Impacts and how technology can help (or hinder) your efforts to meet your community's needs.

Then, we'll walk through our list of generations and note what you can and should do to specifically for each. As in our chapter on the People You Serve, we'll look at five generations rather than three, because it is all five that you will be addressing in your technology planning. We'll also look at some dos and don'ts and suggestions for the organization as a whole.

We'll finish by reviewing yet again our Six Big Actions, since they play into technology very actively. By the end of the chapter, you should have a better idea of how to tackle this ever-changing and increasingly essential part of your organization and its provision of mission.

And, yes, I'll make a suggestion on an iPod policy.

The Four Impacts and Technology

Let's begin our examination of technology and generations by looking at the Four Impacts and their implications. The Boomers dominate, but with technology everyone is a player, either actively or passively. And, while we may (justifiably) assume that the younger we trend, the more comfortable we are with technology, there are dangers to stereotyping, as the following examples illustrate.

> FOR EXAMPLE: I got an e-mail from an eighty-five-year-old friend who had a new digital camera and wanted to send me some of his first pictures. He bought the camera, got home, and found he couldn't read the instruction manual: the type was too small. His solution? Buy a magnifying glass? Give up? Call the manufacturer? No, he went on-line, downloaded the instruction manual, cut and pasted the text he needed into his word processor, and printed it out in large type. Pretty tech savvy!

FOR EXAMPLE: I have a younger friend who is twenty-seven, an author, a minor league baseball player, and an environmentalist. Ivy League–educated, from a wealthy family, he never touches a computer. Ever. He writes his books and essays longhand. He doesn't own a cell phone. Fortunately for him, he graduated before iPods and laptops became required for college students. If I want to get in touch with him, I either call his house (and hope he's home because he doesn't have an answering machine) or resort to snail mail.

While you may think that these men are just the exception to the rule—the statistical tails to the right or left edge of the bell curve—think about it more. Imagine if you tried to dumb down your tech to accommodate the "old folks," and the photographer above figured it out. He'd be (justifiably) insulted, and as we all know, unhappy customers tell twenty other people, usually before they tell you. Do you want that out there?

Imagine that you meet the author/baseball player/environmentalist at a fundraiser and see him as a good future prospect. How would you leave the conversation? "Nice to meet you. If it's OK, I'll e-mail you some materials." Quite possible, because we assume that everyone under forty has (and wants!) access to e-mail. When my friend said, "I don't use e-mail," would you blanch, furrow your brow, or go with the flow?

Here's the point: while technology is a key and growing part of everyday life, it is still a sensitive area in our culture, one that presents us, like any other change, with opportunity *and* danger.

Jim Collins has famously written that successful organizations use technology as an accelerator, not a solution in and of itself. Tech can also be a dividing line, between the haves and the have-nots, the educated and the undereducated, the technophiles and the technophobes, no matter what their age. Notice I did not say the divide between young and old. That's because, while we are at risk in intergenerational applications of technology, we have to seek to break down barriers, be sensitive to different wants, and provide people technological choices.

With that behind us, let's look at the Four Impacts.

Boomers coming in the door

Ah, the Boomers. Look at them: fussing with their PDAs, e-mailing each other bad jokes, fuming about spam, forgetting to upgrade their firewalls, ordering online, never ordering online, saying to each other, "Remember when we used to get actual letters in the mail?" If you have Boomers as employees, governing volunteers, donors, or people you serve (and you almost certainly do), this is a key tech cohort for you.

The most important thing to remember about the Boomers is this: it's a big generation, not only in terms of size, but also in terms of when high tech entered their lives. And in general, the younger you are when you learn a new technology, the more comfortable you are with it.

> **FOR EXAMPLE:** As you already know, I am a Boomer who was born in 1952. I saw my first PC at twenty-eight and had my first luggable (the predecessor of the laptop) at thirty. My wife and I had our first "bagphone" (a five-pound cell phone) when we were thirty-five and got on to Compuserve (the infant Internet) at thirty-three. We were "early adopters" of technology.
>
> There are Boomers who did all of those things for the first time when they were ten years younger or eight years older than me. This is because I was born in 1952, and the birth year of the generation stretches from 1946 to 1962. Thus—and this is important—lots of Boomers saw their first high tech at a younger age than I did, and thus, as a group are more comfortable with it than are Boomers my age or older.

Hence the same caution as in my examples of the Luddite author and technophile octogenarian—trends matter, but so do individuals.

With that said, we go to the accelerator of this issue: boomers all want it their way, hate being thrown into a group. We're very individualistic and very idealistic. And, again, there's lots of us, and for the time being, we have the money.

Boomers going out the door

Lots and lots of tech-savvy Boomers are retiring and these people are gold for you, either as volunteers, or as part time IT managers. *Do not* assume that Boomers cannot code, set up a network, or troubleshoot your server. They can, they love it, and they're out there wanting to help. Combine this skill with the Boomers' delight in having a cause, and you have a nearly perfect match. Skilled Boomers have a ton to offer as second-career employees and/or volunteers.

Whatever happened to GenX and Gen@?

Remember that both GenXers and Gen@s are social creatures; they like to be together. When it comes to technology, GenX and Gen@ are online, or if they're not, they are at least connected to the tech-net by cell phone or PDA. With these people, your first, middle, and last point of contact are going to be in bits and bytes. We'll talk more about this when we go through the generation-specific tech material below, but let me remind you here of this: if you aren't seeing Gen@ or GenX members, whether you need volunteers, donors, people to serve, or employees, you need to rethink the method in which you are contacting them. Considerations:

- Are you looking for employees on Monster.com or craigslist?
- Is your web site complete so that visitors can find everything they need to know about volunteer opportunities?
- Can your board members discuss issues between meetings via an e-mail mailing list?
- Does your web site include educational and background information about your issue or cause?

If the answer to any of these questions is no, you're a nonentity for most Gen@ or GenX members. And being invisible is not a good thing for a nonprofit.

Unintended consequences

Recently a company sent out the wrong e-mail to 10,000 customers—a copy of an e-mail between the company CEO and marketing director, in which the marketing director characterized customers as "idiot children." Whoops. There's a one-click unintended tech consequence.

Unintended consequences show up more frequently the more complex the system is. And tech is complicated. Tech is so pervasive, and has so much to do with our lives, that it has become a system in and of itself.

Certainly the results of not thinking through (and double checking) our tech plans, our tech applications, our tech strategy can have dire unintended consequences.

> **FOR EXAMPLE:** A local church has a link on its web site to a truly bad, bad place, a porn site that is full of viruses and spyware. Why is it there? Because, unbeknownst to the church staff, the link site's domain name, which was formerly used by another faith-based organization, had been bought by the porn site operator. But the key to the story is that the transfer of the domain name had happened a year ago. A year ago—someone wasn't on the ball.

While the porn people play cruel tricks like this regularly, a visitor to the church's web site won't care whose fault it is, and they will be highly offended. As we go through our tech list, we'll deal with this kind of problem, and hopefully avoid other standard unintended consequences.

Let's look at the issue of technology generation by generation.

Technology and Generations

Let's start this section by walking through the tech likes and dislikes of each generation, as well as reviewing the big tech event in each generation's upbringing.

Generational Technology Likes and Dislikes

Think about these in relation to your marketing efforts. Are you feeding the likes?

Gen@ Likes . . .	Gen@ Dislikes . . .
• Instant messaging • Text messaging • Tech support through chat • Researching online • Large-scale online role-playing games (think teamwork)	• Slow response to communications • Insufficient information online • Poor web site design • Lack of access to information • Lack of ability to collaborate, either via in-person involvement in decisions or via tech-enabled teamwork

GenX Likes . . .	GenX Dislikes . . .
• E-mail as primary communication method • BlackBerrys • Shopping online	• Lack of response from superiors to e-mails • Lack of availability of superiors (by e-mail or by cell phone) • Insufficient information online

Boomers Like . . .	Boomers Dislike . . .
• Talking to a live person when the phone is answered • E-mail • Using search engines, but with minimal clicks to find what they need	• Spam • New software, new looks on web sites • New cell phones that do 1,548 things—1,547 of which they don't need • Nonintuitive web sites • Everyone having access to all the information • Being put on hold "because I have another call coming in" • Reading "tiny" print and wading through distracting designs

As you go through the rest of this chapter, think about the different takes the different generations have on technology. How can you use that diversity in your organization?

Technology for Your Nonprofit

A number of tech resources are listed in the Resources section of this book, and more appear on the book's web site, so for now, I'll focus on some technologies that are rapidly spreading at the time this book is being written. Of course, such discussion is fraught with danger: many of these technologies will be old hat by the time you read about them. However, if they are, and you are still not utilizing them, you're even further behind the curve! Let's take a look.

Web sites

Let's start with the assumption that your organization not only has a web site but has been through several versions of that site. Here are things you should consider that attract different generations:

- **Separate parts of your site (password-protected) for board members and staff.** We covered the reasons for this in earlier chapters, but it bears repeating here. For GenX and Gen@ staff members and volunteers, having more information, more forms, minutes of meetings, and names of other staff and volunteers meets their need for everything being on the Net, and for connecting with others online.

- **More educational materials.** Make sure you regularly research and have links to books, CDs, DVDs, web sites, and papers that can educate your users about your cause and the issues surrounding it. This might include links to proposed legislation, research, blogs, discussion groups, and other organizations that may also share your mission zeal. This will appeal to all generations. Some of my client organizations set up information in what they call "The Reading Room." This title alone makes it more appealing to some users.

- **Donations online via credit card and PayPal.** Here is a great example of an option that some people may use, and others won't. The younger you go, the higher the percentage of people paying for things online. What Gen@ members don't do is write checks. So, if you want their money, have this option on your site. While your Greatest Generation supporters will most likely use checks, online payments are still a must in today's competitive fundraising environment.

- **Capacity to review and comment.** A key desire of Gen@ and, to a lesser extent GenX, the availability of a place to comment on the volunteer, staff, donor, and, no less important, the end user's experience is important and no longer particularly technically difficult. It requires some work done on your server or with your Internet service provider, but will pay huge rewards if these age groups are your target market for staff, donors, volunteers, or users. Remember, most Gen@s will not sample your organization if it doesn't come recommended by a peer. So give people the place to comment on and recommend you.

- **Feedback.** Here's another benefit of this kind of space on your web site: immediate feedback. You will get both kudos and criticisms, just as you will any time you ask. You can pass on the kudos and deal quickly with the problems that prompt the criticism.

- **RSS feeds.** RSS (Real Simple Syndication) is a terrific way to keep intermittent web site visitors informed about new things on your web site. Most blogs, for example, allow for RSS feeds so that readers can be informed when a new posting is available to read. Gen@ members are very comfortable with this kind of communication, as long as it doesn't overwhelm them with useless information. Items such as your schedule of volunteer opportunities, new ways of donating, or notices of blog postings are appropriate for RSS feeds.

- **Search.** You can't put all the information you would like on your home page: it's just too confusing. Having a *good* search function on your web site allows your users to find what they're looking for in the magic three or four clicks. You can delegate this to Google, of course, and add a search box, or you can have your own search engine. Make sure the search box is *prominently* placed on your home page and all other pages as well.

Blogs

As most readers know, blogs are shorthand for *web logs,* which at this writing are popping up on the Net by the thousands every day. Some are just personal rants or an accounting of what the author does each day. Many are subject motivated, whether the subject be politics, nuclear power, or nonprofits. If you haven't already done so, you can search to see what blogs are being written about your particular mission issue at either Google (blogsearch.google.com) or Technorati.com.

In generational terms, blogs appeal to GenX and Gen@'s inherent need to be heard, to network, and to get peer opinions. They also can involve more people in your organization and facilitate great feedback from the people you serve. How? Blogs can drive people to your web site, engage them discussing your issue (the blog should allow comments), humanize your issue, and keep people up to date on current happenings in the organization. For example, if yours is a heavily volunteer-driven organization, how about a blog written by one or two regular volunteers who share their insights, experiences, and encourage others to volunteer? If your organization is an animal shelter, how about a blog that notes which pets are up for adoption, and posts pictures, not only of available pets but also of happy people taking their pets home?

Blogs are remarkably easy to start. No extra software is required, just a link to your web site. In addition to Google, which owns Blogger (www.blogger.com), you can use www.writingup.com. (More options are certainly available online if you want to search for them.) But, while starting a blog is easy, keeping it fresh is a discipline, so make sure your authors commit to posting regularly. Looking at a blog with a most recent post that's nine months old is like seeing stale bread.

Blogs are here to stay, at least in some form. They have tapped a deep need in people to connect, and are very efficient at doing so.

E-mail

I know that cell phones are the technology we most love and hate simultaneously, but e-mail is not far behind. E-mail is so ubiquitous now that we have a hard time appreciating what it has done to make our lives easier, our work more efficient, our costs of mailing, shipping, faxing, and telephony go down. That's the good news. The bad, of course, is that e-mail can be a self-enslavement tool, just like text messages on your PDA.

Notice I say self-enslavement. You have to open your e-mail software to allow it to bug you. Some staff may have an expectation of immediate response to an e-mail, but most people, particularly Boomers, don't. E-mail is simple to tame: check it at regular intervals—say 10 a.m. and 2 p.m. rather than at 8 a.m. and noon. You'll get more done, be less depressed, and it will wait for you, just like your paper in box.

Interestingly, e-mail has a generational component as well. It is certainly an expected (and usually preferred) mode of communication for Boomers, but after work hours it is not the top thing that GenX and Gen@ use: they are more into text messaging. And, of course, that may change as more and more functions become available in wireless devices. The point is to pay attention and not assume that your prime communications tool is that of another generation.

Here are some tips on making better use of your e-mail.

- **Install spam filters and virus protection, and update them.** You are going to be communicating with important people: staff, donors, staff, people you serve, staff, funders, staff, and board members. You don't want to send them a virus (hence the virus protection), and you'll have enough to read without going through 300 spam messages a day (hence the need for a good spam filter). Many ISPs now offer built-in spam reduction, which varies in quality. And there are a number of good antivirus programs like McAfee and Norton.

  HANDS ON: When you install virus protection, set it up to automatically update. That way you don't have to worry about remembering to do it and get nailed by some new virus that is making the rounds. Most software will prompt you to take this option: Do it. And, while we're on the subject, if you use Windows, have the Automatic Updates, Virus Protection, and Firewall options ON. In XP, go to Control Panel, click on "Security Center," and check to make sure these options are enabled.

- **Generate lists, but don't share them or abuse them.** Using e-mail lists—for example, of all your board, or of a certain committee, or of past donors—is a great way to benefit from the technology. However, here are a few things to think about as you use your e-mail lists.

  - Make sure you carefully cull your lists. Don't just send everything to everyone.

  - Never put a nonemployee or non–board member on a list without their permission.

  - Never even think about selling your e-mail lists. The little money you may get will be outweighed a thousand times by people who will be angry with you.

  - Don't put your mailing list where everyone who gets the mail can see it. I'm sure you get e-mails where there are twenty, thirty, one hundred addresses in the "To" field. I get a couple that have so many names, I have to scroll down two pages to get to the message. In addition to the annoyance, there's a privacy issue here: you are putting e-mail addresses where everyone else in the list can see them. Some people really don't like that.

    HANDS ON: There's a simple way to avoid this. First, address the message to yourself. (This allows you to confirm that it did, in fact, go through.) Then, put the mailing list title (or all the names) in the field labeled "Bcc," which stands for Blind Carbon Copy. Everyone will get their mail from you, but only their own address will be visible.

- **Don't survey solely by e-mail.** While you can *notify* people with e-mail, always use a link to an HTML survey source, such as SurveyMonkey. Plain e-mail surveys (ones where you click "Reply" and then fill in your answers) are notoriously inaccurate. Don't waste your time, or the time of the people you are surveying.

- **Don't assume everyone likes, or regularly reads, e-mail.** This is an issue that will continue to pop up, particularly in relation to your governing volunteers.

  FOR EXAMPLE: Many executives have shared stories like the following. The exec explains that a few months back, she had decided to use e-mail communications with the board, saving money and time. She sent out an e-mail asking the board if this would work for them, and got no dissenting replies. At the next board meeting, she brought the issue up orally, just to make sure everyone was in agreement. Again, no dissent. So, she limited all her communications to e-mail and phone.

  Two board members (out of fifteen) essentially vanished. They stopped coming to all committee meetings, attended board meetings infrequently, and were nowhere near as involved as they had been over the prior (many) years of their board service.

  To her credit, the exec noticed this and checked. She talked to the board members individually and found that, while they had e-mail addresses (which they had provided to the agency when asked), they really didn't like e-mail. One member checked his e-mail "every few months or so, I don't get many." The other couldn't recall when he last checked his e-mail account.

  Neither member had, of course, seen the e-mail notice about the discussion regarding going to all e-mail communications, and both had missed the live board meeting by coincidence. Both were too polite to ask why they weren't getting their regular mail notices anymore!

- **Check personally with your board (and committees and volunteers) about their use of and comfort with e-mail before you leave people behind unintentionally.**

- **Don't assume that paper is bad.** Some people like stuff in their hands to read. And, some of those people want *you* to print it, not them.

  FOR EXAMPLE: Again, a regular complaint: the executive, or financial manager, or board president decides that the organization can save money on copies and postage if all documents sent to the board and committees are sent electronically. Good idea? Or not. I have heard literally hundreds of stories of volunteers who are upset with the expense of doing their own printing, or don't know how, or run out of toner, or simply come to the meeting unprepared and ask for a paper copy—which the staff has to run around and print at the last minute.

HANDS ON: There's a simple solution to this: Give people the choice. If half the board is willing to print out their materials, you've saved that much in printing and postage fees. Just don't give them the choice by e-mail—they may not read it!

- **Don't leave people on the far side of the digital divide.** Even in today's increasingly wired world, not everyone is online (in early 2003, half the population of the world had yet to make its first phone call). When using e-mail (or depending on web sites, for that matter) think carefully about whether you are excluding people you want to reach.

Scheduling, planning, and project management software

Just a bit on this, and more in the Resources section: a number of great applications are online now that can help you schedule conference calls and meetings. You send potential participants an e-mail, they click the link and fill in their availability online. Use of this kind of software will make your administrative assistant very, very happy. Remember that GenX and Gen@ staff and board members are very used to these kinds of applications: they almost certainly used them in undergraduate school, and may use similar applications (particularly the scheduling variety) in their social lives. On the other end of the generational scale, scheduling applications may confuse some older board members and volunteers, so make sure the applications are "clean" and intuitive to use.

Project management software. This software has come a long way as well, and has tremendous uses if you have big projects running at disparate locations, or say if your planning chair wants to monitor the implementation of your strategic plan online rather than bugging you regularly with a phone call. Today's options are user-friendly, and are usually Internet based, allowing people in many places to view and contribute to them. A current application that is very popular is BaseCamp from 37Signals.

Wikis. Speaking of cool software that younger generations are very, very comfortable with, wikis offer some real benefits. *Wikis* are parts of your web site where people can go and change things at their whim. Sounds bad, right? Not at all. If you haven't already done so, take a look at Wikipedia. com—the largest encyclopedia in the world, generated by users who regularly amend, improve, add, and edit listings. Wikis require some preliminary work on your web site, and obviously should be limited to information and projects where all voices are welcome.

> **FOR EXAMPLE:** Here are things that I know that clients of mine have posted on wikis for their staff or board to comment on and edit: mission statement, organizational values, environmental policies, and employee reward policies. Talk about getting input and ownership! Another great use is the development of FAQs. Instead of you listing the questions and answers, let your users post questions and the answers if they know them.

Open source software. Open source software is defined as software applications (some huge, some tiny) written and checked by volunteers and offered for free online. Open source applications are also regularly updated as bugs are found, or innovations are developed. In general, open source applications are stable, safe, and very flexible. The best known piece of open source is Linux, the operating system that competes with Microsoft's Windows. Linux is the result of millions of person hours of volunteer work from hundreds of thousands of volunteers all over the world. It is very popular for running servers, and is showing up as an option on more and more hardware, even for personal computers and laptops.

But open source is not limited to such high-end uses as operating systems. I have used Firefox, the best open source web browser, for over two years without a problem. Thunderbird, an open source e-mail client, is also available—it's much less bug- and virus-prone than Outlook.

For most nonprofits, open source offer a low-cost/no cost, secure, flexible alternative to traditional software. Don't reject it out of hand. Techsoup.org has some great advice on open source, so start there.

Telephony

Your telephone system is technology—one that, more than most of your technology, really ticks people off. Why? Because of this:

> *"Hello. Welcome to XYZ Nonprofit. We value your call. If you know your party's extension, press it now. If you don't and would like a directory, press pound star two. If you want to hear recorded information about programs, press three. If you are inquiring about upcoming events, press four. If this is an emergency, we're sorry and hope you feel better soon. If you want to talk to a live person, press nine and wait for the rest of your life."*

There is no reader who hasn't experienced frustration with this. And, while voice mail is a great tool, depending on an automated operator can be a big turnoff for people, particularly those who have more trouble hearing, less finger dexterity (to "push 1"), and sometimes even problems seeing their phone keys. (While these problems cross generations, they do increase with age.)

FOR EXAMPLE: An organization that I worked with last year has (or rather had) an answering system that starts like the one above—it's actually where I got the "press pound star two." That's literally what you have to do to dig into the staff directory. Then, you get an instruction to "type in the *full first and last name* of the person you want to reach, using pound for the space between the names." I kid you not. To make matters worse, many of the staff have long names that are not phonetic—some are Thai, Polish, or Ukrainian. Now think about dialing the name into your phone handset! Again, imagine someone with arthritis in their fingers, or poor hearing or eyesight, trying this. And think of someone trying to do it on a cell phone while driving!

HANDS ON: Three suggestions in this area: First, have a real live person answer the phone during regular business hours. People will love you for it. Second, if you have music or a radio station playing when a caller is on hold, pick it very, very carefully. Some radio stations, particularly in the morning hours, use offensive language, and some people find certain kinds of music offensive in general. Third, remember to offer your recordings in more than one language, if appropriate. "Para Español, presione el tres."

Also, remember that many younger-generation staff, volunteers, and service recipients don't have a landline phone, *and have no plans to get one.* So? You can't find them in the phone book. Set up a system to get cell phone numbers right off the bat.

That's a good start for you as you consider your tech and its relation to your different generational groups. For more anal people like me—we need a to-do list. Here it is.

Tech To-Do List

Here's a checklist for you as you work your way through your tech challenges. It's not intended to be all-inclusive, but rather a start. Remember, as you upgrade tech, integrate tech, and use tech, have a tech team (as noted below, composed of people from all generations) help you, give you feedback, and integrate the tech in a good way—not one that turns off an entire generation!

If you are not a high-tech lover by nature, habit, or genetics, make sure you get a copy of *The Accidental Techie*, also published by Fieldstone Alliance. It will help you understand the needs of tech managers and how to talk to your techies. Here's my list.

- **Geek up.** This term comes from my techie son, Ben, who told me while he was in high school that the nonprofits he dealt with needed to "geek up," his term for becoming more tech savvy. I agree. Add technical expertise to your board skill set, and figure out a way to have a very skilled and very dedicated volunteer. (See my suggestion below under "Mentor and discuss among generations" about National Honor Society high school students, or have at least part of a staff person's job be to handle your tech. Again, *The Accidental Techie* is a great resource here.)

HANDS ON: Many local organizations focus on nonprofit tech needs. There may be resources at your United Way, your local community foundation or, if you live in a city with one, at your local management services organization (MSO). There is a link for listings of community foundations and MSOs in the Resources section.

- **Subscribe to Nten and TechSoup.** Speaking of great resources, if you haven't already done so, put this book down, log on to the web, and go to Nten, www.nten.org, and TechSoup, www.techsoup.org. Both these organizations are invaluable resources to the nonprofit community. Go, look, be amazed, bookmark, and subscribe to their newsletters.

- **Have a tech committee.** Tech is more than important enough to have its own committee. This is a way to geek up, too. You can ask outsiders with tech skills to serve on the committee, educate the entire group in new uses for tech in pursuit of your mission, and write your tech plan (see below). Use anyone with tech interest, not just people who talk in Perl (that's a programming language). Why? Because this is not just about hardware and software, it's about using tech to do more mission and, in relation to this book, meeting the needs and wants of a variety of generations. So if you just use geeks, you won't get a wide variety of perceptions. Cast a wide net.

- **Have a regular tech users' focus group.** This is a continuation of my last point in the tech committee area. You need feedback from users, not just geeks, on a regular basis. These might be people who visit your web site, staff who are using your accounting or quality assurance software; any user you can find. Get them together twice a year and talk about ways to make your tech more approachable, less frustrating, and more mission enabling.

- **Have a technology plan.** You are going to be dedicating resources to your technology forever. Money and time will be invested, and, of course, it's your first point of contact for many. So plan it out. To help you get started, there's a great tool on the TechSoup web site. It's a technology planning template, and the URL is listed in the Resources section of this book. Part of your tech plan should cover your tech policies, such as iPod (and any personal music player), Internet usage, e-mail usage, and so forth.

iPod policy: What should your iPod policy be? Music can and does help workers with repetitive or creative jobs. Your younger staff and volunteers will probably have some kind of personal music player and use it a lot. But if they need to be alert to dangers (think driving) or need to respond to coworkers quickly and politely—not after saying "What? WHAT?" and then taking out their earbuds—perhaps you should consider limitations. Some places ban them outright. Some allow workers to use them in certain situations at certain times. My suggestion is to generate the policy with a broad group of staff input, and then, like all policies, post it online, review it periodically, and enforce it!

- **Review and stay abreast of your peer organizations.** This includes all the nonprofits in your community (since you are competing with them for staff, volunteers, and donations) and your mission-peer organizations. Visit their web sites frequently.

  HANDS ON: If your state trade association has an annual conference, suggest to the program committee that there be a tech forum where members can talk about what works for them. This is a great way to get lots of already-tested ideas quickly.

- **Don't equate technology with only bits and bytes.** Technology has many benefits—and one of them is better, more focused, and less expensive printed materials. As you look at ways to use tech better, think about your printer too. It may seem low-tech to you, but it can really accelerate your marketing and communications efforts. Remember, smoke signals were high-tech at one time.

- **Be diligent about security.** Nonprofits are staffed and volunteered by nice people doing nice things for other (mostly) nice people. We forget some days that the rest of the world is not always so nice. Pay attention to security, and pay for it. Look at it like an insurance premium, and don't skimp. It is one area that you need to assign to your best, smartest, most cynical, and most anal IT resource.

Back up, back up, back up. If you don't already do this, investigate online backups. If you back up to disks, or other hard drives, remember to take them offsite regularly. If the office burns down, floods, or is hit by a tornado, all the backups in the world won't help if they were sitting in a drawer next to your computer server.

The Six Big Actions and Technology

Include generational issues in planning

In the tech to-do list above, I advocated both having a tech team and a tech user focus group, as well as a tech plan. In all of those venues, remember that generations look at things differently when confronted with technology. Give individuals the choice of whether or not to use technology, how to use it, and when to use it, to the extent you can. Provide support—to staff, volunteers, and end users—if at all possible. But, like all the other areas we've discussed, keep generational issues in the mix when making plans, setting goals, and allocating funds.

Mentor and discuss among generations

Technology changes very fast, and sometimes too fast for those of us over forty. So, make sure that your tech team (the one I suggested above) is multigenerational, and that they are listening to your technophobic staff and volunteers when you change your web site, update your software, change login procedures, and so forth.

Technology is a great, great place to reverse the standard situation of older people being wiser than younger people. Here you can (and absolutely should) turn traditional mentoring on its head.

In most areas of what we do, we usually think of mentors as older and mentees as younger—if not in age, then in experience. In technology, you turn that on its head. Remember the story about GE's CEO Jack Welch and his young Internet tutor? Use younger mentors.

Those mentors don't have to be staff. They can be volunteers, they can be part of other organizations, and they can be pretty young.

HANDS ON: If your organization is too small (or too broke, or both!) to afford a full time IT person, look to your high schools. Every high school has a chapter of the National Honor Society (NHS) in it. NHS students, all juniors and seniors, are selected for their scholarship, leadership, and community involvement. Being elected to NHS is a benefit for college applications as well as scholarship awards, so the students are motivated to get into NHS and stay in. NHS students must work a certain number of volunteer hours each month, both during the school year and in the summer between junior and senior year.

Go to your nearest high school and ask the principal for the name of the faculty member who advises the NHS students. Find out how to be included on the eligible agency list for volunteers. Then, ask the advisor if you could offer a volunteering opportunity to two of the junior computer geeks. You want two (they work better in pairs) and you want juniors (you get them for two years), if possible.

These young people are dependable, hard-working, and they know their stuff. Many have probably already set up networks for their own homes, in friends' homes, and probably for two or three small businesses. And, best of all, it encourages volunteerism in young people, showing them the rewards of giving up some of their time and talent for the community. One hint: don't just sit them down at your computers and say "Go to it!" Make sure you take the time to show them your mission first so they are working in context and have some idea of the higher calling of your organization.

A couple of cautions about outside tech help, whether it be from high-schoolers or Boomers: geeks like geek stuff. They often, in their urge to help, want to take you into more complex solutions than you need. Technology needs to serve mission, and you should work really hard to avoid being bullied in any way by outside tech volunteers. The coolest application is not always the best, just as the glossy four-color annual report may be appealing to the marketing geek, but offensive to your donor.

Target market by generation

As noted previously, technology accelerates your capacity to target market by generation. You can develop paper materials for technophobes and great web sites for younger or more technocentric users, staff, and volunteers. You can ask (in surveys) by phone, in person, by focused survey, by HTML. Don't always skew your marketing to the highest technology or the lowest. And don't be satisfied with some middle ground of compromise.

Good marketing requires targeting and focusing, and the same holds true for your generational differentiations. Use your technology to focus on them, and you will be much, much more successful.

Age down

In a very real sense, as you geek up, you age down. For most nonprofits, raising the quality and diversity of technology used in the pursuit of mission is a very high need. In expanding your technology use, you can open up better connections with a younger population of staff, board, donors, and volunteers.

Meet techspectations

This entire chapter has been about this subject, so I won't go into great length here, other than to say meeting techspectations is an increasingly important component of customer, staff, and volunteer satisfaction. Ignore this trend at your peril.

Ask

In the technology checklist you saw an item called "Have a regular tech user focus group." This is a good start, but you should include in your culture of asking what we discussed in the marketing chapter—paying close attention to the way people use and don't use your technology.

> **HANDS ON:** As a seasoned nonprofit manager, you already know that measuring is essential to good management. Your web site is one

of those things that needs measuring, and it winds up being a silent form of asking. People vote with their fingers and their mice.

Most Internet service providers (ISPs) have options for your web site to track users, what they look at, how long they stay on a site, what search terms they use. Some ISPs offer a basic set of metrics for free and then a higher-level sorting for a fee. Also, some free online applications do the same thing. Before you go after the information, think about what you want to know. Traffic count is good, but make sure you are spending your time (and possibly your money) on the right things.

Of course, there is more proactive asking than just watching web traffic counts. Observe how staff are using your web site, online forms, financial software. Talk to them when upgrades are installed. Is there a need for more training, if only to make people feel more secure?

Summary

In this chapter, we got you and your organization a bit more geeked up. We looked at the need to resist stereotyping generations in regard to tech, and to really focus on giving people (whether they are staff, board, volunteers, users, or donors) choices that meet their tech needs and wants.

First, we walked through our Four Impacts. Boomers coming in the door mean dealing with a wide range of tech needs and comfort. Boomers going out the door (of their current employer) offer a huge opportunity for experienced tech help.

We then moved to a brief examination of tech by generation, reviewing the biggest tech effect on each group, their likes and dislikes, and some thoughts on how to appeal on a generation-specific basis.

Then we looked at a variety of technology and its uses in nonprofits: web sites (including online payments, commenting and feedback, RSS feeds, and searches); blogs; e-mail; scheduling, planning, and project management software (including wikis and open source software); and telephony.

I proposed a nine-item Tech To-Do list that, while not the be-all, end-all of tech, will get you well on your way. The items on this list include

- Geek up
- Subscribe to Nten and TechSoup
- Have a tech committee
- Have a regular tech users' focus group
- Have a tech plan (including an iPod policy)
- Review and stay abreast of your peer organizations
- Don't equate technology with only bits and bytes
- Be diligent about security
- Back up, back up, back up

Finally, we reviewed the Six Big Actions in relation to technology. Particularly important is the "mentor and discuss" action, which includes ways for smaller organizations to geek up quickly and inexpensively.

Technology is, and will continue to be, a great mission accelerator. Fraught with both infinite promise and immense peril, it must be shaped for use in your organization in the coming years, no matter what mix of age groups you appeal to. The true digital divide is going to show up as a chasm between nonprofits that get this and those that don't. Don't be on the wrong side of this divide.

That said, remember that with technology, the simple solution—the one that supports your mission the most closely—is often the best.

Now that we've discussed technology, we have only one more subject to think about: money. Boomers coming in or out—there will be financial implications. Funding going up or down—there will be financial implications. GenX staff wanting more flexible benefits? Again, financial implications. Looking at these issues and all kinds of other money matters is the subject of our next chapter.

CHAPTER EIGHT DISCUSSION QUESTIONS

1. Do we have an adequate technology committee on staff? How can we expand it to represent generational issues?

2. Does our technology plan consider diversity of generations in addition to other diversities?

3. Do we check our web site for currency, and compare it to other peer organization web sites every six months?

4. Is there a use for podcasts for staff training, for orientation, or for education of users online?

5. What about blogs? Do they make sense for us to use, given that they need regular contributions?

6. Are we sensitive in our use of tech to older eyes and ears?

7. Do we have an iPod or IM policy? Do we need one?

9

Financial Implications

NO MONEY, NO MISSION. Whatever your generation, this rule pertains. While "Mission, mission, and more mission" is the first rule of nonprofits, "No money, no mission" is a close second. Without financial resources, no mission flows. As a good steward of your nonprofit's finances, you need to take a look at how generational change will affect your organization's finances. This makes sense on a number of levels because, as we all know, you push down one place and something else pops up, sort of like the Whack-A-Mole game kids play at arcades.

In this chapter, we'll examine financial implications, actions, and ideas related to generational change. As before, we'll start with the Four Impacts and how they relate to financial planning. Then we'll look at some specific income and expense items to consider, including pensions, insurance, flex benefits, and the like.

After that, we'll look at your balance sheet. Is it strong enough? Can you afford debt? What if you need to take on debt to allow Boomers to retire sooner? Should you increase your line of credit? Are your ratios in line? I'll give you some specific ideas to start with immediately.

Next, we'll examine perhaps the biggest issue with Boomers—that of retirement. This has huge implications for your financial situation, and I'll show you how to deal with it head on, starting now. Finally, we'll finish up by looking at the Six Big Actions, and how you can tune them to the financial side of the mission/money balancing act.

By the end of this chapter you should have a pretty good handle on the effect of generational change on your organization.

The Four Impacts and Finance

Money matters, even if we don't want to admit it. Money matters differently to different people, and even differently to the same people in different situations. While we all may want to think that mission is the *only* thing for our organization, it's really just the first thing, with the "No money, no mission" rule coming right behind.

In looking at our Four Impacts and financial implications, we have to keep in mind the different generational financial values and widely varied situations that generations are in, because there are differences. I am not going to argue that Boomers care less about money than GenXers, or vice versa, but it is a fact that many Boomers are caught in the financial vises of caring for elderly parents while putting children through college, and that hundreds of thousands of Gen@ people come out of college and grad school with educational debt that's several times greater than the cost of the first house Boomers purchased.

Boomers coming in the door

Accommodation. More than anything, a herd of aging Boomers coming in the door, particularly as people to serve, requires accommodation. A lot of it. And accommodating costs money. Whether it is larger-print options on marketing materials, higher average lumens in your waiting areas (to accommodate older eyes), warmer offices to accommodate older workers who tend to get cold easily, or the traditional ADA type accommodations of ramps, bathrooms, and so forth (which you all should have, but may need to expand), accommodation equals expenditure.

The Boomers who are already on staff, or who are joining the staff as second-career transfers, also are going to stretch your finances in terms of retirement needs, health care premiums, life insurance premiums, and so forth. In Chapter 4, I suggested that you look at the retirement plans of your management team and other Boomers. Here is where you can put the financial spin on that information.

Again, the key here is focus and flexibility. We'll talk about that more below as we look at your income and expense statement and your balance sheet.

Boomers going out the door

If you work for me, and you are sixty-three and I assume you are going out the door to retirement in two years, I'll gauge my financial planning for salary, health insurance premiums, 401(k) contributions, and sick time accordingly. But if you surprise me and stay more five years, it can really throw my numbers out of whack. This is why you need to talk to your Boomer employees early and often about their retirement.

The other issue with Boomers going out the door and your finances is the potential of traditional donor Boomers retiring and leaving your community along with their regular donations (and matching donations from their employers). If you are located in a retirement mecca, more Boomers are moving in than out, but for the rest of the world, this is going to be a problem. And even if the Boomers aren't moving away, retirement always brings with it some financial reevaluation. Retirees nearly always think through their priorities, and if your organization is not a top priority to them, you may fall off the list.

Whatever happened to GenX and Gen@?

Where did the young people go? In terms of finances, they got buried under school debt. I mentioned this earlier, but it is such a huge social and financial change that it bears some greater focus. In the chapter on staff, I told you about my Kellogg students who want to work for nonprofits but can't afford to because they have to pay off their enormous college debts.

What are the financial implications of this? If you have or intend to have a greater number of younger employees with higher ed backgrounds, you almost certainly will get some with school loans on their minds. This will affect their willingness to work for you at whatever salary you can offer. But if you engage them knowledgeably about the issue, and you (or your HR people) know some options for helping with loans, you may be able to show yourself as a sympathetic, concerned employer.

> **HANDS ON:** Knowing about paying for college is also a key issue for any employees you have who are parents and want to know more about their choices. Think about having an expert speaker come in to

talk to your parent employees. Offer employees a list of places to go to learn more about government programs and other strategies for paying for college.

Unintended consequences

I've seen this story play out countless times over the past ten years. A great exec, one who watches every dime the organization spends, intentionally does not have the agency make any agency contribution to her retirement any time the budget is not great. The exec does this out of the goodness of her heart. "It's more important to do services." But she does it year after year, and suddenly she is sixty and there isn't enough in her retirement account. What has happened? By being selfless and dedicated, the exec (and her board) have severely limited the options open to the agency as it plans for its next generation of leadership. They have potentially *hurt the mission*. They've forgotten the rule of compound interest—that a little contribution now pays off big as the years roll by. Their intentions were only the best. The unintended results are limited choices, all very expensive.

Income and Expense Issues

Most nonprofit managers are very familiar with their budget and the resulting income and expense statement. Even executives who only learned about finance after they got into their current position understand the basic mechanics of this report and its implications. Money in, *good*. Money out, *bad*. Right?

Not so fast. Nonprofits need to think of their expenses as *investments in mission*. Then a bad thing—spending money—becomes a potentially very good thing, something that should result in more mission being produced. So, as we look at your income and expense statement, try to think of it in this newer, more optimistic way.

We'll deal with this financial statement in order, first looking at the effect of generational change on income, and then on expenses. Essentially, I'll be giving you a list of things to consider, examine, research, and estimate as you plan.

Income

Generations can do a number of things to your income statement, some good, some not good.

Your organization's capacity to adapt to generational change affects its income. If you follow the advice in this book and adjust your services (for example, proactively adding or changing services that meet coming population changes), fundraising approaches (for example, adding PayPal and online donations), and marketing (for example, providing both print and online brochures) to accommodate generational change, your organization's revenues should do just fine. You'll be meeting wants by generation, and revenues should continue coming in or even improve. Fail to plan for these changes, and the bad results are easy to predict.

You may Compete with Boomers for government dollars. You really can't control this issue. You can and should advocate, of course, but in any event you need to plan for it while you work to influence local, state, and federal policy. Unless you are targeting seniors, the Boomers (by reason of their numbers and the fact that people tend to vote more as they get older) will be taking the lion's share of federal and state dollars with them as they age out.

Thus, organizations that focus on issues unrelated to Boomer's median age (children's issues, for example) will likely be competing for fewer government dollars. The result will be a limited financial "pie" for non-Boomer services, and fierce competition for remaining governmental funds. Here, honing your marketing well in advance plays a key role. Additionally, building up your balance sheet, specifically your cash-on-hand, is a good idea.

Finally, if your organization has not adapted a proactive public policy stance, now is the time. You can work through both the legislative and executive branches to influence how much money is available for your cause. Sure, Boomers will be consuming government funds for health care, assisted housing—you name it. But those Boomers will have grandkids, and your legislators and executives (who will be GenXers) will have kids, and if your issue is helping children, you can be fighting hard for the piece of the pie that those kids need to thrive in the future.

This is not going to be a one- or two-year glitch. It might be more like a twenty- or perhaps thirty-year hit—so prepare for it.

MeBranding is the future. Ignoring MeBranding can cause a serious hit to your income stream, particularly if you serve a younger audience or client set. First, focus on your target markets, and then find out what people want. Then give them as many choices as possible—or at least as many choices as you can *afford*.

For many organizations, the costs of providing more options will outweigh the income increases. Your hope here is to just break even, and even that may have to be weighed over more than just one fiscal year.

The Boomers are moving out (or in) with their donations. Pay close attention to your fundraising income stream. Categorize it by generation and find out if any of your larger annual donors are planning to move out of town to a retirement mecca. You can't predict every move of every donor, but asking doesn't hurt, and you can then begin to assess the likelihood of a donation that has come in every year for the last ten years continuing for the next ten.

Expense

Here are some things related to generational change that may well affect your expenses in the next few years.

Retirement funding for workers of all ages. As noted earlier, you will likely have to increase your retirement contributions. (More about that in relation to Boomers shortly.) You should be planning for all your employees, from Gen@ on up. In fact, GenX members have heard the warnings about the end of Social Security in their lifetimes and are more concerned about their long-range future than Boomers have been.

While you might feel that your organization can't afford to contribute to employee pension or retirement accounts, the least you can do is educate your employees as to their options and help them set up 403(b), 401(k), or IRA accounts.

HANDS ON: Nonprofits have a moral imperative to help their employees with retirement. We already underpay and overwork most of our employees in relation to what they could earn in the private sector. Matching employee contributions to an IRA, 403(b), or 401(k) account up to a set limit (and, of course, within the law) is the right thing to do, and it encourages staff members to think out into the future. Make sure your retirement contribution match formula is the same for every full-time employee. Don't favor management, particularly the executive director.

HANDS ON: The starting point is to offer educational sessions on retirement beginning now, and recurring annually: perhaps a brown bag lunch series or an evening event open to all employees. Use this regular event as a starting point for more discussion about retirement plans.

HANDS ON: Be careful who you choose to do the educating. Financial planners are in business to sell their pension, insurance, and other products. Try to get a neutral party, and don't bring them into a large group unless you have heard them speak yourself.

Higher salaries for higher educated workers. Here's an issue that may well sneak up and bite you. The younger (GenX and Gen@) managers coming out of undergraduate and graduate school with degrees in nonprofit management may well require higher pay than their less-schooled peers. While you may feel that everyone should be paid the same, the market disagrees. You are competing not only against other nonprofits, but also against for-profit employers. A student coming out of a graduate program at Yale, Northwestern, Stanford, Johns Hopkins, or the University of North Carolina, to name only a few, has the ticket to work in either world. Further, while these students may *plan* to work in nonprofits, they may well not be able to afford to. Their student debt may well preclude any thought of taking a lower-paying (and yet more satisfying) job. Paying them at a higher rate will help them defray their additional costs in education.

For this very reason, wages (and all the concomitant fringe costs) will probably rise faster in our sector than in others. Nonprofits have a lot of catching up to do.

Flexible benefits. GenX and Gen@ workers need (or want) flexible benefits. Flexibility may well mean more expense to the employer, and this needs careful checking and regular bidding of your benefits package.

> **HANDS ON:** For most nonprofits, employee benefits are a big part of overall expenses. This is nearly always a large enough expense to bid periodically. (I recommend every three years.) The field (and pricing) changes fast enough to merit regular reviews. Make sure you get references from other customers. Customer service when you have a need or a claim is crucial. And remember, each bidding cycle is an opportunity to go back and ask your employees what they prefer in a benefits package. No sense in getting bids on benefits people don't want, or have moved beyond.

Flexible benefits are probably already offered to some degree in your organization (with flex plan withdrawals from employees' paychecks). But you should consider going further—the market of GenX and Gen@ employees wants you to.

Cost of part-time workers. Part-time workers may earn less, but they don't necessarily cost less. Not only is their tax cost higher up front (they won't max out their annual Social Security contribution, for example), but the cost of insurance (if you offer it), training, and the initial investment you make is higher relative to the hours worked than with a full-time person. (Of course, if you don't offer health care or other benefits to your part-timers, or offer widely different benefits, then the numbers change.)

Which is not to say that part-timers aren't valuable—they are. They may be less prone to burnout, they often bring an intense energy to work and, if they requested part-time rather full-time work, they are often very happy campers.

HANDS ON: If you haven't used part-time workers before, or if it's been a few years, before you offer such work to any current employee, make sure you brush up on state and federal law regarding all the rules and regulations that apply to this kind of worker. There are points (in hours per week) where you must offer benefits. Also, check your benefits packages to see whether you can offer full coverage to part-timers. Do your homework before you dive in.

Fewer full-time workers. Another hit to your expenses may come from losing the "efficiency" of Boomer full-time employees (FTEs) in terms of their cost per actual hour worked. As most readers know, many salaried workers work far more than the required hours. This is particularly true at the higher management levels. Here's the dilemma, which we've discussed a few times earlier. If younger managers are more interested in work-life balance, and are not working the hours that their predecessors did (for, perhaps, excellent reasons), how is the work going to get done? While some work can simply be done faster, some can't. For example, if you provide 24/7 services you must have staff available 24/7.

Will this result in a larger number of FTEs for you? Maybe. Will those FTEs cost more if the workers are younger? Maybe, maybe not. It all depends on your particular organization—but it is absolutely essential to start looking at this.

HANDS ON: Remember that for most nonprofits, over 80 percent of expenses are tied up in personnel. Kick up your people costs 5 percent and you take a real ding. Take a look around at the marketplace, ask peer organizations what they've been paying for new employees, and get educated.

Boomer retirement will be the biggest potential short- and long-term hits on your expenses—so potentially huge as to merit its own section (next).

Retiring the Boomers

If your staff are the usual mix, some of your Boomers are wanting to retire but haven't a clue what their financial situation is. Others have done multiple estimates and watch their retirement funds daily, hoping to reach that mythical amount of money at which they can cut and run.

The retirement of your Boomer staff will affect your finances. Why? Because research shows that most employees are underfunded for retirement. Is this the nonprofit's problem? Shouldn't these individuals have put more away?

Well, it might be the individual's problem—but it is also yours. In some cases, nonprofit staff have been systematically underpaid and nonprofits have been slow to support any form of retirement. And there's also the situation (discussed in Chapter 5) wherein the board is afraid to let go of the executive who is past her best service but lacks retirement funds. This last situation sometimes ends in the deadly scenario where a board, to ease an executive transition, pays the former executive a consulting fee for a few years to do some work around the agency—which invariably sabotages her successor.

Quick-funding a pension. There is no truly good solution to quickly fund a pension or retirement package. For one thing, federal law specifies how much you can contribute annually to a 401(k) or 403(b) plan. But there are many other options, as any financial planner will tell you. One agency I worked with took out a loan to fund a pension and at the same time took out life insurance on the executive, the proceeds of which will be used (at her death) to pay off the loan. (It wasn't perfect, but it enabled a fair solution that did not break the bank.)

> **HANDS ON:** If you are in this situation, get at least three different bids. Sit down with your executive staff one by one (remember, this is not just a CEO issue) and talk about the date of their retirement and their financial needs. Provide those parameters to the financial planners and see what they come up with. Remember to look at all the organizational costs over the life of the plan. The longer you've waited to get on this, the more it will cost you: compound interest works a whole lot better for you over twenty years than twenty months.

Remember in your pension and retirement planning to work with your Gen@ and GenX staff who, in general, are much more cognizant of this issue at an early age than their Boomer peers were (and are).

The Six Big Actions and Finance

Our Six Big Actions have much to show us in relation to financial issues. Let's walk through them for the last time and see how we can use them to do better planning, get more information, and be better financial stewards.

Include generational issues in planning

Planning is an essential part of a well-run organization, and nowhere is this more critical than in regarding finances. You are probably pretty skilled at budgeting, one form of financial planning. Now you need to develop some spreadsheets that look at your finances with a longer horizon—ones that anticipate the effects of generational change on your organization. You need a ten-year financial impact plan related to generations. A good spreadsheet file is the key here—one that is flexible enough to accommodate your organizations' specific needs.

Once you find out who is retiring when, you can look at the cash impact of paying them for accrued sick leave and vacation. Once you see what younger staff want in terms of flex benefits, you can plug that in. Will younger staff work fewer hours? How much will that cost in part-time staff? What about reduced income from donations as retiring Boomers move away? Make an entry for that. Have some Boomers committed funds to your planned giving program? Enter those. Go back through this book and look at the financial impact of technology, staff, volunteers, marketing, MeBranding. Don't leave anything out.

HANDS ON: Put together a financial impact group that includes your banker, your auditor, your treasurer, and perhaps a professional financial planner (someone who advises people on their investments and retirement). All of these people are dealing with this same issue with lots of for-profit businesses. They can bring that expertise to the table for you and your organization.

HANDS ON: Look to see whether anything is being done in this area by your state or national trade association. Have peer organizations gotten a handle on this issue?

Mentor and discuss among generations

Follow through with suggestions to initiate discussions and find out staff retirement goals. The same goes for volunteers, particularly if they are involved in direct service.

Establish some mentoring in the area of retirement planning. We talked about this in the chapter on staff, but the sooner the entire staff (including the management team and executive director) take on responsibility for their own planning and retirement, the less guilt the board will feel about any underfunding that may have occurred in the past. And then everyone can make a more accurate measure of "the number" that they will need to retire.

The same kind of mentoring should go on regarding student loans of your younger staff. A little education and support goes a long way in this area.

Target market by generation

In the financial area, flex benefits are a great example of how you can meet wants by generation. If you have a truly flexible benefits plan (which we discussed in Chapter 4), you can offer the same overall cost to employees (depending on whether they are full time or part-time) but let them choose *how* to spend the money. You can also offer other benefits that don't come as part of a normal insurance/benefits package, such as educational support in both time and tuition.

HANDS ON: Remember in developing flexible benefits to pay attention to both federal and state laws, as well as any collective bargaining agreement you may be subject to. Also, your younger employees may opt to carry less insurance than your older ones (because they think they are immortal) but don't let them opt for no insurance. Set minimums, and educate them about the importance of having at least catastrophic coverage.

HANDS ON: One change in benefit terminology I see more and more is the removing of the terms "sick," "personal," "vacation," and the like from the area of time off. The rationale is that if you trust your people, they shouldn't have to bring a note from the doctor if they or their child (or parent, or spouse, or favorite aunt who has no one else) is sick. Boomers tend to minimize their use of "sick" time, but they will take personal time. And, as the Bard put it, "What's in a name?" Time is time. So set the *amount* of time people can take off, and how it is earned (usually by length of service, monthly, quarterly, or annually) and go from there.

HANDS ON: One *relatively* simple benefit is a sick bank. Here, employees can contribute one or more days a year to the sick bank, which other employees can use (with permission from an employee committee or HR) if they have a major issue to deal with. For example, when my father-in-law was diagnosed with a terminal illness in 1999, my wife, Chris, went to be with him and help him through his final two or three weeks. Key word: weeks—that's what all of us were told. Her dad lived for a bit over two months, and Chris had only accumulated sick leave of just over ten days. But her faculty has a sick bank, and approved her drawing from that. Talk about team building!

Age down

Financially, aging down has mostly to do with employees. And younger is usually cheaper. But, as I noted above, *as generational groups,* Gen@ and GenX are less likely to want to contribute as much unpaid overtime (for salaried workers). This is not to say they don't work hard, because they do. And it's not to say that they won't put in overtime, but it isn't assumed the way it was for the Boomers. As these generations start to have families, work increasingly takes a back seat to family. Thus, just getting the work done may take more FTEs and more expense than you are used to. In addition, aging down may well require a rethinking of flex time, sick time, parental leave, and vacation time, to say nothing of paid benefits—all to accommodate the needs of younger full- and part-time employees. The costs can go up, go down, or stay the same. And, as always, some of the benefits can't be counted.

> **FOR EXAMPLE:** An executive of a nonprofit in the desert Southwest wrote to me after a posting on my blog about this issue. The organization has five FTEs in its accounting office, consisting of eight people (six of whom work part-time from home). The employees in question are mainly mothers of small children who hated their commute and wanted to be home when their children get home from school. One by one, they talked to their boss about leaving, and she saw the writing on the wall. "These employees were excellent, experienced, and hard-working, but their home situations had changed. I didn't want to risk losing them, so we figured out how to parcel out their work so that they could do it at home. They have to come into the office at mid-day one day every two weeks for a face-to-face staff meeting. We even moved the time of the meeting to accommodate their children's school schedule. We needed to make some software and security changes, and our tech guys were busy for a week or so moving the employees' computers home and making sure that their online access was fast and secure. But, the overall benefit has been huge. The employees are ecstatic, and we use the space they used to occupy for other pressing needs, avoiding renting additional space."

Meet techspectations

Techspectations in the money area are many. An important one is that financial information will be available online. Whether it is budgeting by a Gen@ staff member, or looking at retirement information for a Boomer, the increasing expectation is that this information will be available at the touch of a keypad. But security is crucial, so don't do one without the other.

If you haven't yet gone to direct-deposit payroll for staff, start. In my interviews with Gen@ members, I asked them if they had direct deposit or took home a paper paycheck. *One hundred percent* of them had opted for the direct deposit. Why? "Less chance I'll lose the check." "I have access to the money right away." "I can just go to the ATM," were the answers.

Techspectations also show up for donors too. More and more they want to donate online by credit card and PayPal. You've already heard my admonitions about this, but consider another common type of payment—electronic check. These checks can show up in two forms: electronic deposits from some banks, and paper checks from others. In both cases, you need to make sure your accounting system and staff are prepared to give proper credit for tax deductions, as well as place the donations in any restricted funds the donors choose consistently. This is not high tech, but it certainly is fraught with danger in terms of donor satisfaction if you mishandle the donation.

Ask

Keep communications open. Talk to people, ask in surveys, have brown bag lunches, conduct focus groups. The same admonition I've tossed at you throughout the book returns for one last engagement here: Ask. Don't assume. Respect people enough to get their opinion. Ask. Forewarn yourself and your organization. Of all the areas that we've covered, the one that enables all the others is *money*. Without it, you can't accomplish your mission, hire staff, train volunteers, buy and use tech, or serve the community. Asking people so that you know more about the financial implications of their plans, their actions, and their generational perspectives is good management and good stewardship. To paraphrase an old saying, "The only dumb question is the one that doesn't get asked." Ask.

Summary

In this chapter, we've dealt with generational finance issues in some detail. You've seen how to get ahead of the curve in financial planning, how to predict the effect of generational change to a certain degree, and how to keep lines of communication open about money issues, which is always a challenge.

We looked at the Four Impacts—the financial implications of Boomers in, Boomers out, younger generations and their crushing school debt, and the unintended consequences that show up in large social change.

We examined some specific issues, including income and expense and balance sheet effects. These included

Income effects

- Your organization's capacity to adapt to generational change affects its income
- You may compete with Boomers for government dollars
- MeBranding is the future
- The Boomers are moving out (or in) with their donations

Expense effects

- Retirement funding for workers of all ages
- Higher salaries for higher educated workers
- Flexible benefits
- Cost of part-time workers
- Fewer full-time workers

We turned to the financial side of the retirement of the Boomers, a huge issue for every nonprofit. Finally, we explored the Six Big Actions as they relate to finance, and looked at the development of a ten-year generational financial impact plan, to be updated every two years.

I suspect you've heard enough about money for a while, and probably wish you could just focus on more mission without worrying about financial issues. But remember what I said at the beginning of the chapter: "No money, no mission." Like so many issues in the nonprofit world, this is a balancing act. If we focus too much on money, and not enough on mission, we become just a regular business; if we focus too much on mission and forget or ignore the money side, we go out of business and don't provide mission to anyone. So money matters, in generation planning as well as in regular day-to-day stewardship.

CHAPTER NINE DISCUSSION QUESTIONS

1. How are we preparing for the retirement of our current workers? Have we educated them enough? Is there more we can afford to do financially?

2. How should we start developing our ten-year financial impact plan?

3. Are our benefits flexible enough for our Gen@ and GenX workers? How much is this going to cost us over time?

4. What financial metrics should we use or adjust as we head into generation change?

5. Should we offer financial planning education for all our employees? What would their expectations be?

6. Can we offer any help to younger employees in relation to their school debts? Longevity bonuses?

Final Words

THE TITLE OF THIS BOOK notes that generational change is the challenge of a lifetime. I believe that, and hope by this time that you do too. Pay attention to the suggestions in this book that work for your organization, listen to your different generations speak, watch for things through generation-sensitive eyes, and you and your organization will be fine.

Unless . . .

- Unless you let generational issues distract you from your mission.

- Unless you perseverate so much on executive transition, or paying for Boomer retirement, or aging down your board, that you lose the focus on your most important resource, the resource that is even more important than your staff and volunteers, no matter what their age—your mission.

Your mission is and must remain the most important thing in your organization. If it does, you will carry on a great tradition.

- Mission worked for the Greatest Generation. They won a world war and built the greatest economy the world has ever known.

- Mission worked for the Boomers. We changed the world forever.

- Mission is working for GenX and Gen@ even though they are just getting started. I can't wait to see what they'll make of their mission and their contribution to our communities.

Finally, if we all do our job right, if we all stay true to our missions, then our organizations will be in place to help the *next* generation, and the next, and the next.

And you know what's great? Mission will work for them too.

Peter Brinckerhoff

Springfield, Illinois
August 2006

Resources

THE CHAPTERS THAT YOU'VE ALREADY READ have provided you with ideas, suggestions, conundrums and, hopefully, a call to action on generational change in your organization. They should get you started. This chapter provides resources that will help you customize your response to generational issues in your organization.

The chapter is divided into two main areas. First, all the discussion questions for the previous chapters are aggregated here. Readers of earlier books said such a compendium would help them see all the issues at once and would help when leading discussion groups.

Next comes a wide variety of print and web resources. The book references are straightforward, but the web sites and the discussion papers (and their associated URLs) are, as always, fraught with the possibility of change between the time of publication and the time you try to type them into your browser. If you can't find them, try searching on a few of the key terms.

Discussion Questions Review by Chapter

Chapter 4: Generations on Staff

1. What does our staff age breakout look like? How are our generations on staff changing?

2. Do we need to collect or update our staff satisfaction information? Do we have adequate data on work-life balance?

3. How can we establish a mentoring program? Do we have enough staff turnover to merit this investment?

4. Do we see intergenerational conflict now? If it is present, how can we reduce it or prevent it in the future?

5. Are we doing enough asking in generational groups? What can we do better in this area?

Chapter 5: Board and Volunteers

1. Do we have a good age diversity and representation on our board and in our volunteers? How can we do better?

2. How can we keep the pipeline of younger volunteers full? Who do we need to be in touch with—high Schools, colleges, military organizations, church youth groups?

3. What can be done to accommodate our older board members and volunteers as well as our younger ones? How can we give both a sense of community?

4. What about mentoring on the board? How can we use that with our other volunteers, and perhaps with our new staff?

Chapter 6: The People We Serve

1. How do our services break out generationally? Do we collect adequate information to know, or do we need to estimate?

2. What's happening in the population in our community? Is our community (or our constituency) aging quickly, getting younger, trading generations?

3. What do our service recipients tell us about ways we can improve? Is there an age component to these suggestions?

4. Are we asking our customers what they want often enough? Too often? Are we asking in enough different ways? Are we really listening to what they are telling us? How can we connect better?

5. Are there "hidden" customers whose age is changing? For example, the parents in the co-op preschool who needed stools?

Chapter 7: Marketing

1. Should we use the marketing cycle to reevaluate our marketing in light of generational change?

2. Do we need to look at our target markets again? Who are they, and do they break out by generation? How? Should we rework our marketing plan?

3. Do we need to reexamine how we get our message across through various technologies to ensure that we are not excluding or turning off any generational group?

4. What about the tech vehicle of our asking? Is it effective, or do we need to plan and implement some changes?

5. Are we really *listening* to every generation or are we just asking? How can we tell?

6. What are two or three ways we can specifically accommodate to MeBranding? Which market should we look at first?

Chapter 8: Technology

1. Do we have an adequate tech committee on staff? How can we expand it to represent generational issues?

2. Does our technology plan consider diversity of generations in addition to other diversities?

3. Do we check our web site for currency, and compare it to other peer organization web sites every six months?

4. Is there a use for podcasts for staff training, for orientation, or for education of users online?

5. What about blogs? Do they make sense for us to use, given that they need regular contributions?

6. Are we adequately sensitive in our use of tech to older eyes and ears?

7. Do we have an iPod or IM policy? Do we need one?

Chapter 9: Finance

1. How are we preparing for the retirement of our current workers? Have we educated them enough? Is there more we can afford to do financially?

2. How should we start developing our ten-year financial impact plan?

3. Are our benefits flexible enough for our Gen@ and GenX workers? How much is this going to cost us over time?

4. What financial metrics should we use or adjust as we head into generation change?

5. Should we offer financial planning education for all our employees? What would be their expectations?

6. Can we offer any help to younger employees in relation to their school debts? Longevity bonuses?

Print and Web Resources

Books

Bennett, Sue, with Tom Battin, et al. 2005. *The Accidental Techie: Supporting, Managing, and Maximizing Your Nonprofit's Technology.* St. Paul, MN: Fieldstone Alliance.

Chait, Richard, William Ryan, and Barbara Taylor. 2004. *Governance as Leadership: Reframing the Work of Nonprofit Boards.* Hoboken, NJ: John Wiley & Sons.

Hicks, Rick, and Kathy Hicks. 1999. *Boomers, Xers and Other Strangers: Understanding the Generational Differences That Divide Us.* Wheaton, IL: Tyndale House.

Howe, Neil, and William Strauss. 2000. *Millennials Rising: The Next Great Generation.* New York: Vintage Books.

Karp, Hank, Connie Fuller, and Danilo Sirias. 2002. *Bridging the Boomer Gap: Creating Authentic Teams for High Performance at Work.* Palo Alto, CA: Davies-Black Publishing.

Kotter, John, and Dan Cohen. 2002. *The Heart of Change: Real-Life Stories of How People Change Their Organizations.* Boston: Harvard Business Press.

Kouzes, James, and Barry Posner. 2002. *The Leadership Challenge, 3rd ed.* San Francisco: Jossey-Bass.

Lancaster, Lynne C., and David Stillman. 2002. *When Generations Collide: Who They Are, Why They Clash, How to Solve the Generational Puzzle at Work.* New York: HarperCollins.

Martin, Carolyn, and Bruce Tulgan. 2002. *Managing the Generation Mix: From Collision to Collaboration.* Amherst, MA: HRD Press.

Raines, Claire. 2003. *Connecting Generations: The Sourcebook for a New Workplace.* Menlo Park, CA: Crisp Publications.

Zemke, Ron, Claire Raines, and Bob Filipczak. 2002. *Generations at Work: Managing the Clash of Veterans, Boomers, Xers, and Nexters in Your Workplace.* New York: AMACOM.

Discussion papers

Kunreuther, Frances, for Annie E. Casey Foundation. 2005. "Up Next: Generation Change and the Leadership of Nonprofit Organizations." Available online at http://www.aecf.org/publications/data/up_next.pdf.

Salls, Manda, and Susan Moses. 2004. "The Nonprofit Boon From the Boomers." *Harvard Business School Working Knowledge for Business Leaders.* October 18. Available online at http://hbswk.hbs.edu/archive/4416.html.

Web sites

American Demographics. Great site for trends by age group:
www.adage.com/americandemographics/

Congressional Budget Office outlook on Boomer Retirement:
www.cbo.gov/showdoc.cfm?index=5195&sequence=0

Nten Tech Resources for Nonprofits:
www.nten.org

Population Reference Bureau page for diversity in generations:
www.prb.org/Template.cfm?Section=PRB&template=/
ContentManagement/ContentDisplay.cfm&ContentID=10201

Preparing for Baby Boomer Retirement:
www.clomedia.com/content/templates/clo_article.asp?articleid=
976&zoneid=24

Retirement Guide for Nonprofit Employers:
http://philanthropy.com/jobs/2003/05/15/20030515–135487.htm

TechSoup.org:
www.techsoup.org

Transition Guide information for leadership change:
www.transitionguides.com/

U.S. Census main page. A terrific resource:
www.census.gov

Index

More results-oriented books from Fieldstone Alliance

The Manager's Guide to Program Evaluation:
Planning, Contracting, and Managing for Useful Results
by Paul W. Mattessich, PhD

Explains how to plan and manage an evaluation that will help identify your organization's successes, share information with key audiences, and improve services.

96 pages, softcover   Item# 069385

New Americans, New Promise
A Guide to the Refugee Journey in America
by Yorn Yan

Author Yorn Yan, a refugee from Cambodia, describes the refugee experience in the United States and how to best help refugees through the acculturation and transition process of becoming a New American.

200 pages, softcover   Item# 069504

The Nonprofit Mergers Workbook
The Leader's Guide to Considering, Negotiating, and Executing a Merger
by David La Piana

Save time, money, and untold frustration with this highly practical guide that makes the merger process manageable and controllable.

240 pages, softcover   Item# 069210

The Nonprofit Mergers Workbook Part II
Unifying the Organization after a Merger
by La Piana Associates

Once the merger agreement is signed, the question becomes: How do we make this merger work? *Part II* helps you create a comprehensive plan to achieve *integration*—bringing together people, programs, processes, and systems from two (or more) organizations into a single, unified whole.

248 pages,with CD-ROM   Item# 069415

Nonprofit Stewardship
A Better Way to Lead Your Mission-Based Organization
by Peter C. Brinckerhoff

The stewardship model of leadership can help your organization improve its mission capability by forcing you to keep your organization's mission foremost. It helps you make decisions that are best for the people your organization serves. In other words, stewardship helps you do more good for more people.

272 pages, softcover   Item# 069423

Resolving Conflict in Nonprofit Organizations
The Leader's Guide to Finding Constructive Solutions
by Marion Peters Angelica

Helps you identify conflict, decide whether to intervene, uncover and deal with the true issues, and design and conduct a conflict resolution process. Includes exercises to learn and practice conflict resolution skills, guidance on handling unique conflicts such as harassment and discrimination, and when (and where) to seek outside help.

192 pages, softcover   Item# 069164

Strategic Planning Workbook for Nonprofit Organizations, Revised and Updated
by Bryan Barry

Chart a wise course for your nonprofit's future. This time-tested workbook gives you practical step-by-step guidance, real-life examples, one nonprofit's complete strategic plan, and easy-to-use worksheets.

144 pages, softcover   Item# 069075

Finance

Bookkeeping Basics
What Every Nonprofit Bookkeeper Needs to Know
by Debra L. Ruegg and Lisa M. Venkatrathnam

Complete with step-by-step instructions, a glossary of accounting terms, detailed examples, and handy reproducible forms, this book will enable you to successfully meet the basic bookkeeping requirements of your nonprofit organization.

128 pages, softcover   Item # 069296

Coping with Cutbacks
The Nonprofit Guide to Success When Times Are Tight
by Emil Angelica and Vincent Hyman

Shows you practical ways to involve business, government, and other nonprofits to solve problems together. Also includes 185 cutback strategies you can put to use right away.

128 pages, softcover   Item # 069091

Financial Leadership for Nonprofit Executives
Guiding Your Organization to Long-term Success
by Jeanne Peters and Elizabeth Schaffer

A practical guide to protecting and growing the assets of your organizations and accomplishing as much mission as possible with those resources.

144 pages, softcover   Item# 06944X

For current prices, a catalog, or to order call 800-274-6024

Venture Forth! The Essential Guide to Starting a Moneymaking Business in Your Nonprofit Organization
by Rolfe Larson

The most complete guide on nonprofit business development. Building on the experience of dozens of organizations, this handbook gives you a time-tested approach for finding, testing, and launching a successful nonprofit business venture.

272 pages, softcover   Item# 069245

Marketing

The Fieldstone Alliance Nonprofit Guide to
Conducting Successful Focus Groups
by Judith Sharken Simon

Shows how to collect valuable information without a lot of money or special expertise. Using this proven technique, you'll get essential opinions and feedback to help you check out your assumptions, do better strategic planning, improve services or products, and more.

80 pages, softcover   Item# 069199

Marketing Workbook for Nonprofit Organizations Volume I: Develop the Plan
by Gary J. Stern

Don't just wish for results—get them! Here's how to create a straightforward, usable marketing plan. Includes the six Ps of Marketing, how to use them effectively, a sample marketing plan, tips on using the Internet, and worksheets.

208 pages, softcover   Item# 069253

Marketing Workbook for Nonprofit Organizations Volume II: Mobilize People for Marketing Success
by Gary J. Stern

Put together a successful promotional campaign based on the most persuasive tool of all: personal contact. Learn how to mobilize your entire organization, its staff, volunteers, and supporters in a focused, one-to-one marketing campaign. Comes with *Pocket Guide for Marketing Representatives*. In it, your marketing representatives can record key campaign messages and find motivational reminders.

192 pages, softcover   Item# 069105

Community Building

Community Building: What Makes It Work
by Wilder Research Center

Reveals twenty-eight keys to help you build community more effectively. Includes detailed descriptions of each factor, case examples of how they play out, and practical questions to assess your work.

112 pages, softcover   Ite# 069121

Community Economic Development Handbook
by Mihailo Temali

A concrete, practical handbook to turning any neighborhood around. It explains how to start a community economic development organization, and then lays out the steps of four proven and powerful strategies for revitalizing inner-city neighborhoods.

288 pages, softcover   Item# 069369

The Community Leadership Handbook
by Jim Krile

Based on the best of Blandin Foundation's 20-year experience in developing community leaders—this book gives community members 14 tools to bring people together to make change.

240 pages, softcover   Item# 069547

The Fieldstone Alliance Nonprofit Guide to
Conducting Community Forums
by Carol Lukas and Linda Hoskins

Provides step-by-step instruction to plan and carry out exciting, successful community forums that will educate the public, build consensus, focus action, or influence policy.

128 pages, softcover   Item# 069318

The Creative Community Builder's Handbook
How to Transform Communities Using Local Assets, Art, and Culture
by Thomas Borrup

Creative community building is about bringing community development, arts and culture, planning and design, and citizen participation together to create sustainable communities. This book provides examples and tools to help community builders utilize human cultures and the creativity in everyone.

272 pages, softcover   Item# 069474